Energy Security

Asia Pacific Perspectives

Attention Authors

Manas Publications is fighting a war to tell the world that India can win the battle not only by the bullet but also by the pen. We are converting fighters into writers. There is no dearth of intellectuals in our country, however, their knowledge is confined to them only. No sincere effort has been made by any other publisher to give the right direction to their knowledge and the talent of every intellectual is lying hidden. An author always presents the raw material in the shape of a manuscript and it is the job of the publisher to convert it to a finished product. Manas has been continually motivating intellectuals and publishing their manuscripts for more than two decades and would like to publish your manuscript too. If you or your colleagues have a manuscript ready for publication or are working on it, contact us with a detailed synopsis and list of contents. Manas will also suggest you a suitable title for writing related to your area of expertise. Manas is known for its publishing quality. We take utmost care in publishing and also give wide publicity to the book and its author through our national and international distribution network.

Energy Security
Asia Pacific Perspectives

Editors

Virendra Gupta

Chong Guan Kwa

Associate Editors

Dr. Bhupendra Kumar Singh

Consultant (Energy Security), MEA

Dr. Alvin Chew

Youngho Chang

Manas Publications

New Delhi-110002 (INDIA)

Manas Publications
(Publishers, Distributors, Importers & Exporters)
4402/5A, Main Ansari Road,
(Opp. HDFC Bank), Darya Ganj,
New Delhi - 110 002 (INDIA)
Ph.: 23260783, 23265523:, 23842660 (R)
Fax: 011-23272766
E-mail: manaspublications@vsnl.com
website **www.manaspublications.in**

2010

ISBN 978-81-7049-355-6
Rs. **495/-**

Typeset at
Manas Publications

Printed in India at
Jaico Printers, Delhi
and Published by Mrs Suman Lata for
Manas Publications, 4402/5A, Main Ansari Road,
Opp. HDFC Bank, Darya Ganj,
New Delhi - 110 002 (INDIA)

Contents

Notes on Editors/Contributors

Virendra Gupta, IFS

After short stints with State Bank of India and Indian Forest Service, he joined Indian Foreign Service in 1977. Has served in various diplomatic positions in Indian Missions in Nepal, Nigeria, Israel and Egypt as well as Permanent Mission of India to UN in New York prior to his assignment as Indian High Commissioner in Tanzania (1998-2001) and Trinidad & Tobago, West Indies (2001-2005). He has also served as Deputy Director and South Asia Cluster Coordinator at the country's premier think tank, Institute of Defence and Strategic Analyses. After successfully completing the term as Additional Secretary Investment, Trade Promotion and Energy Security in the Ministry of External Affairs, currently he is Director General of Indian Council for Cultural Relations.

Dr. Bhupendra Kumar Singh

Ph.D on Energy Security from Jawaharlal Nehru University (JNU), New Delhi, he has written many articles in reputed Journals and Newspapers. His article "India's Energy Security", published in *The Hindu* has been quoted by Bruce Vaughn in "Indian Geopolitics, the United States and Evolving Correlates of Power in Asia", *Geopolitic, 9 (2)*, 2004. His paper "India's Energy Security: A Comparative Analysis of Petroleum and Nuclear Energy" was declared as the Best Research Paper in Indian Social Science Congress for the Strategic and Defence Studies. He got laurels for his paper "Energy Security and India-China Cooperation", presented at 2nd International Association of Energy Economics Conference, Perth (Australia) on 7 November 2008. Recently he has written a chapter along with Virendra Gupta, titled "Energy Security Imperatives in South Asia", in South Asia Defence and Strategic Year Book 2009. Currently he is a full time Consultant (Energy Security), Ministry of External Affairs, Government of India.

Chong Guan Kwa

He is Head of External Programs, S Rajaratnam School of International Studies, Nanyang Technological University and an Adjunct Associate Professor at the Department of History, National University of Singapore. He was previously Head of the SAFTI Military Institute's Department of Strategic Studies which he helped establish and concurrently, Adjunct Associate Professor in the Division of History of the National Institute of Education's School of Arts. Before joining the SAFTI Military Institute, Mr Kwa served in various capacities in the National Heritage Board, the National Museum and the Oral History Center. He continues to be associated with their institutions through their advisory committees. Mr Kwa started his working career in the Ministry of Foreign Affairs before being posted to the Ministry of Defence. He was commissioned into the Singapore Armed Forces in 1969 and had served in a variety of reservist command and staff appointments upto Division level.

Youngho Chang

Dr Chang is an Assistant Professor in the Division of Economics at S. Rajaratnam School of International Studies, Nanyang Technological University, Singapore. He is also an Adjunct Senior Fellow at the Energy Studies Institute, National University of Singapore and a member of R&D Workgroup and Household Subcommittee for the National Climate Change Committee.

Michal Meidan

Michal Meidan is a research associate at Asia Centre à Sciences-po where she heads the activities of the Energy and Environment programme. Her research focuses on China's energy policy and decision-making. She is a PhD Candidate at Sciences-po, Paris, and holds an MA in Political Sciences and East Asian studies.

Jor-Shan Choi

Dr. Jor-Shan Choi is a Professor for the G-COE Program of the Department of Nuclear Engineering and Management at Tokyo University, Japan. Before that, Dr. Choi had 21 years of working experience at Lawrence Livermore National Laboratory (LLNL) in California, USA. In 1995-96, he was a Science Fellow at the Center for International Security and Cooperation (CISAC) at Stanford University. He also worked for the International Atomic Energy Agency (IAEA) in Vienna from 1998-2001. Prior to joining LLNL in 1987, Dr. Choi had 13 years of industrial experience working for Bechtel. He has a PhD in Nuclear Engineering from the University of California at Berkeley. He is also a registered Professional Engineer (PE) in the State of California.

Yuji Morita

Mr. Yuji Morita graduated from the University of Kyoto, Organic Chemistry in the Department of Science in 1974. He joined the Institute of Energy Economics, Japan in 1998. As Senior Research Fellow and Director of the Energy Data and Modeling Center, his responsibility covers project management for various kinds of research on energy.

Dr. Chung-young Chang

Dr. Chung-young Chang is a full-time professor at the Department of Public Affairs of Fo-Guang University in Taiwan. He has published several books and a number of articles in various periodicals on the following topics: *Intelligence and National Security, National Security Establishment, Non-Traditional Security Studies and Crisis Management*.

Dr. Frank Umbach

Dr. Frank Umbach is currently Senior Associate of the Centre for European Security Strategies (CESS) in Munich, Berlin and a Consultant on International Energy Security. He's a regional expert on energy, foreign and security policy in East Asia, Russia, the Caspian Region as well as EU and NATO – i.e. of energy supply security, energy foreign policies, geopolitical challenges and global energy trends.

Zhou Xingbao

Mr. Zhou Xingbao was born in 1941 in Shanghai, China. After graduation from Beijing University of Foreign Studies as a research student, he joined the Ministry of Foreign Affairs in 1965. In 1973 he joined China Institute of International Studies (CIIS). Since then he worked as a researcher, Associate Research Fellow and Senior Research Fellow and Vice President of the Institute. He also worked as First Secretary in the Chinese Embassy in U.K. and the Chinese Consul General in Toronto. Since 2001, he has been Senior Research Fellow, CIIS and Vice-Chairman and Secretary General, CSCAP China.

Zhao Hongtu

Dr. Zhao is a research professor of China Institute of Contemporary International Relations (CICIR). He has been visiting fellow at the University of Wisconsin-Madison and Energy Charter Secretariat. His research interests are Energy Security, Energy Diplomacy, International Energy Cooperation and Climate Change.

Dr Alvin Chew

Dr Alvin Chew is a Research Fellow at the S. Rajaratnam School of International Studies (RSIS) and the co-ordinator for the Science, Technology and Security Programme in the school. His research interests include the broad areas of energy security and specialises in the developments of nuclear energy in Southeast Asia.

Talmiz Ahmad

Talmiz Ahmad was appointed India's Ambassador to the UAE in August 2007. After obtaining his Master's degree in History, Mr. Ahmad joined the Indian diplomatic service in 1974, and served in the countries of the Arabian Peninsula, including Kuwait, Iraq, Yemen and Saudi Arabia. He also served in the Indian diplomatic missions in New York, London and Pretoria. He was the Spokesman of the Ministry of External Affairs in 1997, after which he headed the Gulf Haj Division in the Ministry (1998–2000).

Mr. Ahmad was the Indian Ambassador to Saudi Arabia (2000–2003) and Oman (2003–2004). As Additional Secretary in the Ministry of Petroleum and Natural Gas (2004–2006), he was responsible for handling India's diplomatic effort in the area of energy security. He was the head of India's premier foreign policy think-tank, the Indian Council of World Affairs (2006–2007).

Jae-Seung Lee

Jae-Seung Lee is currently Associate Dean and Associate Professor at Korea University, Division of International Studies. As a scholar in international political economy and policy advisor to the Korean government, Jae-Seung Lee has worked on regional cooperation and energy security and has recently published a number of books and articles on these issues.

Andrew Forbes

Andrew Forbes is a Visiting Senior Fellow at the Australian National Center for Ocean Resources and Security at the University of Wollongong; a Research Fellow at the Center for Foreign Policy Studies at Dalhousie University, Halifax, Canada; and is the editor of a number of books on maritime security issues.

Foreword

Energy Security: A Study by Council for Security and Cooperation in Asia-Pacific (CSCAP)

Energy security is a global preoccupation today. With rapidly growing energy demand spurred by rising economic growth, especially in the emerging economies the need for uninterrupted and reliable energy supplies at competitive prices has multiplied as never before. At the same time the extraordinary dilemma that is presently faced is how to strike a balance between the exponentially increasing energy consumption on the one hand and the worrisome challenge of climate change on the other.

Energy security has been defined variously and each country or region has its own ideas or policies to tackle this priority concern. In the vast and diverse region of the Asia-Pacific which is home to half the world's population and which is expected to be the driving force for realizing the ambition for the 'Asian century' the energy scene is assuming a critical dimension. This region is characterized by high consumption as well as large scale production. The distribution of energy resources in the region is also uneven and the question of energy independence or interdependence continues to loom large in making the policy choices. At the same time, the role of technology has become highly significant since it is recognized that ultimately it is the technology that can make a huge difference to our knowledge about the availability of energy resources and the ability to harness them.

It is on this complex background surrounding the energy issue that the Council for Security and Cooperation in the Asia-Pacific (CSCAP), a leading non-governmental forum in the Asia-Pacific took the initiative in December 2006 to set up a Study Group on Cooperation in Energy Security in the Asia-Pacific. Singapore accepted the Chairmanship and India was the Co-Chair. This book is the outcome of the deliberations in the Study Group held over past two years in which a number of papers on the diverse questions relating to energy were presented. It is gratifying to find that CSCAP decided to bring these discussions in the form of a book. In doing so, they have tried to place before the international community a whole range of energy issues confronting the Asia-Pacific and an array of possible policy options. It is a matter of deep satisfaction for the Indian Council of World Affairs, New Delhi which works closely with the CSCAP India Chapter to publish this book.

Clearly, today there is no one country, no single multinational corporation nor one single technology which can find answer to the twin challenges of energy security and climate change. The imperative logic, therefore, is for cooperation, including among the consumers and producers. This is by no means easily attainable just as energy independence too is an elusive goal. Search for energy independence can lead to severe competition, if not tension among nations threatening a major conflict. After all, for any nation the need for energy is immediate and paramount. On the other hand, cooperation among nations in the area of energy is a goal not entirely unrealistic. Today enlightened self-interest is driving nations to accept that they would need other states to strike an optimum balance in their pursuit of energy security. Consumers require producers and vice versa. Both need technology from private or public enterprises. The need of the hour is to forge cooperation through R&D collaboration, technology sharing, market reforms and infrastructure development. All this can be done in a spirit of interdependence. A meeting was held in January 2005 in New Delhi at which Ministers and high-level representatives from consumer nations such as China, Japan, Korea, ASEAN and India had met with their counterparts from Saudi Arabia, Kuwait, Iran, the United Arab Emirates and the Central Asian states to discuss the issues such as the demand and supply of energy, pricing and exploration opportunities. It would be useful if such interaction among the consuming and producing nations can continue in the future. Interestingly, the issue of impact of energy consumption on environment and the resultant climate change has brought the nations of the world in another dialogue.

The CSCAP Study Group had considered the issue of energy security from a variety of angles—geopolitical, economic, infrastructure-related, technological, energy saving-wise, etc. They have come out with insightful conclusions drawn by experts and scholars. While it is argued that the changed political scenario is affecting the very concept of energy security, it is also pointed out that the economics of energy security suggests a transition to a renewable capital-based economy as the solution for ensuring energy security. Specific energy security concerns have also been discussed in the context of the importance of the Malacca Straits as a principal waterway for energy supplies or threats to energy infrastructure security in the energy supply chain. The role of technology as a tool to address the issue of energy security has also been emphasized. Indeed the concept of energy conservation and efficiency involves the advent of technology to lessen the demand for fuel resources. In this regard the role of nuclear power in relation to energy security also becomes important and a question is raised as to what are the technical, institutional and societal issues that need to be resolved. Specific country/region perspectives from China, Australia, the European Union, Northeast Asia provide useful insights in the situation of energy security in the respective country/region. The EU energy policies and its supply security strategies as also the EU debates on its energy security can be of relevance and interest to the Asia-Pacific region even though the situations in the two differ in many ways. The principles that led to the integration of the European energy market and European energy policies may have a useful lesson to other regions including the Asia-Pacific.

The CSCAP study on energy security is coming out at a time when the global economy faced with the financial crisis is going through a critical phase. With falling GDP growth rates and exports, declining employment and reduced investments, any uncertainty and insecurity on the energy scene would be yet another severe factor for the world economy. The analyses and insights in the area of energy security that this book provides will therefore serve as a useful basis for strategic thinkers, academics and policy makers to examine the issue of energy security from diverse and useful perspectives. The authors of this study have thus made a valuable service in that regard.

Sudhir T. Devare

Director General,
Indian Council of World Affairs,
New Delhi, India

Introduction

In the last couple of years energy security issues have been driven centre stage on the international agenda. This period has witnessed sharp price volatility. Oil prices have now fallen to nearly 1/3rd of the peak levels reached just about a year ago and this raises serious questions about continued investments into the oil and gas sector. We have to recognize that the supplies are finite and that it is only a matter of time that demand begins to put pressure on supplies and consequently the prices unless additional capacities were brought on board in a steadfast and uninterrupted manner. The most critical issue for us, therefore, is to guard against any complacency and to ensure continued flow of investment in upstream oil infrastructure. Concomitantly, the international community must also continue to pay increased attention to the development of renewable sector despite questions about its economic viability the short term.

It is also extremely important that both consumers and producers engage in a close dialogue and transparent exchange of data for developing a cooperative framework in order to calm the markets and to impart the required stability. We have to also proceed with our efforts to develop greater connectivity in the market place. This would involve laying of new pipelines across the continents, connecting different regions and sub-regions. Given the huge financial outlays, however, it is only obvious that due diligence is undertaken covering all issues including those of law and order and security for the requisite comfort level of investors and other stakeholders.

As far as Asia Pacific region is concerned, energy security emanates from the growing imbalance between the demand for energy and its supply from indigenous sources resulting in increased import dependence. The demand for commercial fuels throughout Asia Pacific has risen dramatically. The growth of transportation facilities has had a strong impact on oil consumption, which remains the main source of fuel for the transportation sector. Given huge net deficit of energy resources Asia Pacific countries face mounting energy import bills. The challenge that Asia Pacific countries face is to secure sustainable and affordable energy supplies to meet the ever increasing demand for commercial energy, in particular to ensure access to the general mass.

CSCAP Energy Security Working Group which was set up in 2006 to deal with the above issues held four meetings in Singapore (April 2007), India (September 2007), China (March 2008) and Brunei (July 2008). A number of extremely useful and well-researched papers were presented at these meetings and by all accounts our deliberations contributed to better appreciation of each others perspective. Keeping in view their continued relevance, some of the presentations made at the meetings have been developed and updated further and are being compiled in this volume. We are confident that this publication would prove helpful to the government officials and scholars alike in better understanding of the energy security issues as they affect the countries of Asia and Pacific.

In the Chapter *Reflections of the CSCAP Study Group on Energy & Security*, Chong Guan Kwa examined the underlying motivations in forming the study group to assess the intricate links between energy and security issues, primarily on the two aspects of 'why' and 'how' energy supplies can be secured. The assessment led to the understanding on several nations pursuing the various policy options of energy independence, which loops back to the fundamental impetus of developing an alternative policy approach based on cooperation and coordination of energy supplies among nations to avoid the possibilities of conflicts. In the proposed policy framework of energy inter-dependence, the working group also suggested the expansion of the conventional factors of security and stability in energy supplies, to include the element of sustainability whereby clean and alternative fuel sources can be employed for future energy use.

Chapter on *Australian Energy Security: The benefits of self-sufficiency* by Andrew Forbes describes Australia's energy production and current consumption. Though Australia is generally self-sufficient in energy resources particularly coal, gas and oil, the major problem Australia faces is that except coal, the majority of energy resources are found in remote locations, incurring significant distribution costs. Therefore, some energy resources are imported because it is cheaper to import product than transport energy supplies around Australia. Australia's energy security involves three concerns: security of offshore energy infrastructure, protection of Australian seaborne energy flows and protection of global energy flows. It outlines Australia's energy trade to highlight the linkages between countries for economic, energy and national security. It also analyses security issues associated with protecting Australia's offshore energy infrastructure, Australia's energy trade, and global energy trades. It concludes with ideas on how navies might cooperate to protect seaborne trade.

Chapter on *Europe debates its energy security: Any lesson for Asia?* by Michal Meidan evaluates the European energy security debates. Traditionally European vision of energy security places markets at the forefront of energy interactions. The focus of energy policies in the EU was on integrating energy markets, enhancing and securing physical interconnectivity, as well as achieving a more environmentally friendly growth path. However, the market approach and the liberal rationale were challenged by a number of key events like the Californian energy crisis in 2000, the September 11 attacks and the ensuing turmoil in the Middle East, the emergence of Russia as a strong producer country that fully uses its energy resources as a political tool, seemed to herald a new era in which supplies could no longer be left to the markets. Therefore, this chapter addresses the following questions: what were the underlying principles that guided the integration of the European energy market and European energy policies? What are the new challenges facing Europe and how have they shaped the continent's evolving approach to its energy security? How is this relevant to Asia and what are the implications for future cooperation between Asia and Europe?

In the Chapter, *Malacca Straits and China's Energy Security*, Zhao Hongtu describes about "Malacca dilemma". "Malacca dilemma" states that the deep reliance on Malacca straits and possible oil embargo by United States make China's sea energy life line extremely vulnerable, and their solution relies on developing alternative mainland pipelines and expanding naval force to safeguard the energy shipments in emergency. This chapter examines this dilemma. The author argues that with the development of globalization and ever-increasing economy interdependence between China and the U.S, it is unlikely that the U.S. would impose oil blockades on China. There are many technical obstacles; first, to block or attack oil tankers on the sea, it's very difficult to judge the oil tankers owned by China or hired from other country. Second, blockage of choke points like Malacca Straits will also block the energy transportation of Japan and Korea. Third, about one quarter of world merchant ships carry the products that are made in China. Technically it's difficult to block China's oil tankers without affecting world trade. And also, once there is a blockage or sanction, it will be developed into economy or trade blockage rather oil or energy blockage only. This chapter concludes that "Malacca dilemma" is overstated.

Chapter on *An Assessment on Energy Infrastructure Security* by Chung-young Chang evaluates the importance of energy infrastructure security (EIS), examines the threats to energy infrastructure security and suggests solutions to the threat. Energy infrastructure security is receiving greater strategic and security attention at national, regional and global levels. The primary task of EIS has to safeguard the physical safety and security of tangible properties of energy supply chain such as drilling facilities, refineries, pipelines, oil tanks, storages and control centres. In addition, the security of information and communication technology serving the purpose of control and command energy supply is also crucial to the protection of EIS.

Chapter on *Energy and the Global Political Scenario* by Talmiz Ahmad analyses the global energy scenario after the September 11 attack on World Trade Tower. It tries to explain that how changed political scenario is affecting the very concept of energy security. The author shares the view that the United States has embarked on a strategy of building a new empire in which the control of the Middle East is a prerequisite, Iraq is a cornerstone and Iran remains the major obstacle. US "empire-building" policies in Iraq and attempts to dominate West Asia strategically are being played out in a global environment that is in considerable flux, with the principal players pursuing a number of regional initiatives in support of their strategic interests, largely tied to energy security considerations. The trilateral Russia–China–India dialogue is an attempt by the principal players in Asia to identify and pursue matters that promote their strategic, primarily energy-related interests. Asian countries should pursue its energy interests through cooperative ventures that include investments in upstream and downstream hydrocarbon projects, sustainability proposals and infrastructure projects, particularly transnational pipelines.

Chapter on *EU-Energy Policies and its Supply Security Strategies: EU-Russian Energy Partnership versus Pipeline Dependencies* by Frank Umbach tries to analyse the European Union Energy policy and its dependence on Russia for the supply of energy sources. EU's energy policy has three major components: security of supply, competitiveness and environmental sustainability. The European Commission's energy demand management strategy has always emphasized the diversification in energy supply, promotion of renewable energies and a neutral look at the nuclear option. In regard to the EU's future energy supply security, the expansion of natural gas as an environmental clean energy source will play the most problematic factor in the next two decades for the EU member states. By 2030, Europe would have to import 488 billion cubic metres, if the gas demand would not be mitigated. In many ways, Russia seems to be the natural energy partner for the EU. Given the political instabilities in the Middle East, the natural solution for Germany and the rest of the EU seems to be to expand imports of oil and natural gas from Russia for satisfying its rapidly growing energy demand. The author has opinion that Russia's approach has been most visible in its efforts to undermine a common European policy toward Central Asia. Moscow tries to torpedo the Nabucco-pipeline project, which is of crucial importance for European energy autonomy and the diversification of energy supply, with a rival pipeline ("White Stream-pipeline") and to maintain as well as to strengthen its gas pipeline monopoly from Central Asia to the EU member states. The resulting pipeline rivalry in Central and South Eastern Europe between the EU and Russia has led to increasing tension between the recognized need for a common EU energy and gas market and individual EU member states acting in their own declared long-term energy security interests.

In the Chapter *China's Recent Efforts in International Energy Cooperation,* Zhou Xingbao describes the Chinese energy security strategy based on six specific principles. With its fast growing economy, China has become a big energy consumer in the world. China is also a big energy producer in respect of coal. This chapter basically describes its efforts of international energy cooperation and highlights the six principles on which China would like to ensure its energy security. The six principles are as following. First, both energy exploitation and energy conservation are to be emphasized but priority is given to energy saving. Second, China will continue to rely mainly on its domestic energy supply. China's domestic energy supply still has very great potentials. Third, diversified development of energy sources will be pursued. Fourth, reliance on science and technology will be emphasized. Fifth, China will protect the environment in its energy development. And, sixth, China will promote and strengthen mutually beneficial international energy cooperation.

Chapter on *The Economics of Energy Security*, Youngho Chang defined energy security as an adequate and reliable supply of energy at a reasonable price. Following this definition, the economics of energy security examines the economic consequences of volatile oil prices and the effectiveness of mitigation measures mainly for oil-importing countries. The stylized impacts of high oil prices are slowness in economic growth, a higher inflation and an increase in unemployment. Apart from the energy security for oil-importing countries, the energy security for oil-exporting countries in specific and depletable resource-based economies in general requires those economies to prepare for both the ultimate depletion of resources and the eventual loss of customers. A transition to a renewable capital-based economy is suggested as the solution for ensuring energy security.

In the Chapter *Political Economy of Energy Cooperation in Northeast Asia* by Jae-Seung Lee, he highlighted that there has been extensive energy cooperation in Northeast Asia, owing to the energy crisis in the Middle East. However, the geopolitical structure of Northeast Asia would hinder Northeast Asian energy cooperation. To promote the energy cooperation in Northeast Asia, he recommended policies to enhance bilateral relations in Northeast Asia including China, Japan, Korea and Russia. In addition, the expansion of the geopolitical scope of energy cooperation to East Asia and the Asia Pacific is also recommended. He also underlined the importance to link energy and regional cooperation multilaterally, and to focus on the soft cooperation agenda such as enhancing energy efficiency and strategic reserve and joint R&D projects.

The Chapter on *Energy Security: The Role for Nuclear Energy* by Jor-Shan Choi, he mentioned that the growth in global energy demand and the increased recognition of environmental impacts of greenhouse gases emissions have made many countries turn to the nuclear power option in favour of conventional fossil fuels. Inevitably, concerns over safety and waste management arise, in addition to problems of nuclear proliferation. The author explored the range of issues associated with nuclear power and highlighted that new nuclear power plants must satisfy a number of well-described criteria in terms of being economical, safe, proliferation-resistant, minimization of waste production, and also acceptance by the public community. He is optimistic that with the combination of new reactor technology and coordinated global fuel cycle services, nuclear power can prove to be a viable source to meet future energy demands.

Chapter on *Energy Saving in the Japanese Industrial Sector and International Cooperation,* Yuji Morita highlighted the case study on Japan's drive towards energy conservation and efficiency. Energy saving has been promoted in the country's industrial sector as a lesson learnt from two major oil crises. In order to maintain international competitiveness of its manufacturing products, the nation has introduced energy saving technologies such as Coke Dry Quenching in its iron and steel industry. Such technologies are enhanced and promoted at the international level, with the hope that its introduction will help to reduce carbon emissions.

Finally, in the Chapter on *Technology Developments in Energy Security* by Alvin Chew, he emphasized that technology has been employed as a tool to address the issue of energy security. Developments are carried out in the field of oil exploration to assess the quantity of available oil resources on our planet. In the arena of alternative fuel resources, considerable efforts have been invested into developing renewable energy sources that will have lesser impact on the environment. Technology is also being developed and employed to secure the transportation of fuel resources. The author introduced the concept of energy conservation and efficiency, which involves the advent of technology to lessen our demand for fuel resources, and suggested that while technology is expensive, it is in the interest to foster cooperation among the various developed and developing nations for the transfer of technology.

1

Reflections of the CSCAP Study Group on Energy & Security

Chong Guan Kwa[1]

Concerns about the security of our supplies of energy, principally oil, looms large on the radar screen of policy makers today. However, it may be useful to remind ourselves that it is not a recent concern. Sixty-six years ago Japan felt compelled to invade Southeast Asia in part to gain

---

[1] I stress that these "Reflections" are my personal reflections of the CSCAP Study Group I was privileged to Co-chair with CSCAP-India. I have learnt much from my Indian Co-chairs and other CSCAP participants in this Study Group who cannot be held responsible or associated with any of the views reflected here. I thank my CSCAP-Singapore colleagues, Dr Alvin Chew and Dr Chang Youngho for their inputs into the drafting of these reflections. They also cannot be held responsible or associated with any of these reflections.

access to the region's oil and other strategic staples in the face of a United States embargo on its export of strategic necessities to Japan. Allied victory against both Japan and Germany by contrast was ensured by an adequate supply of oil and the deployment of nuclear power, the legacy of which we live with today. More recently, we remember the consequences of the Organization of Petroleum Exporting Countries' assertion of its control over the supply of oil in support of the Arabs in the 1973-74 Arab-Israeli war.

Current concerns about the security of our energy supplies stem from a variety of more complex causes. In large part they stem from concerns about uncertain and possibly diminishing fossil fuels because of the increasing energy demands of a globalised economy, especially in the Asia Pacific, after the end of the Cold War. In part it also stems from OPEC's more systematic and disciplined regulation of oil prices after 2000. Today concern about the impact of our growing consumption of fossil fuels on our environment drives our search for alternative and hopefully, more sustainable energy sources to reduce our dependence on fossil fuels.

In response to these escalating concerns about the security of our energy supplies, CSCAP in 2007 initiated a Study Group on Energy & Security co-chaired by CSCAP-Singapore and CSCAP-India. The underlying intentions of the Study Group were first to inquire how energy and security were being linked, specifically why we are making supplies of energy a security issue. Second, the Study Group hoped to elucidate the nature of the linkage we are making between energy and security. Third, the Study Group intended to examine the responses and policy options being proposed to ensure the security of our energy supplies. Implicit in the Group's examination of policy options is the assumption that many states and their national governments would be driven by their national interests to attempt to control and confine supplies of energy and accept that challenges, competition and possibly conflict with other states are a consequence of this imperative to control and confine energy supplies. However, CSCAP, as its name indicates, is biased towards strategies which promote cooperation and coordination of our securities over our energy supplies and its deliberations were thus oriented towards framing policy arguments for cooperation and coordination of our energy supplies to avoid possible conflict. It is with this ultimate intent that the Group hoped it could make some policy recommendations about how to frame the policy options that would work towards cooperation and coordination of our energy needs.

1.1 Why is Supply of Energy a Security Issue? The Securitisation of Energy Supplies

One conclusion emerging from the Study Group's deliberations, unsurprisingly, is that how we defined the link between our energy supply and our security depended in large part upon *where* we stand in the spectrum of "supplier" and "consumer" of energy. The post-Cold War opening up and globalization of not only the Chinese and Indian economies, but other Asia Pacific economies have created a demand for an adequate, reliable and affordable supply of energy and countries feel vulnerable if this cannot be assured. In this context, China's surging demand for energy to power its economic take-off has come in for close examination. Is China pursuing control and confine strategies to ensure an adequate and reliable supply of energy for its needs? Our CSCAP-China colleagues stressed that China is committed to cooperative strategies to ensure an adequate, reliable and affordable supply of energy in a globalised and increasingly interdependent world. China, our CSCAP-China colleagues assured, is also committed to more efficient and sustainable use of its energy supplies.

In contrast to the dilemmas of the "consumer" countries, the rising price of oil has made "supplier" countries like Canada into possible "economic powers" because exploitation of its reserves of oil-sands could be economically feasible if high oil prices such as over $100 per barrel are sustained. Likewise with Australia, its coal and uranium reserves may further Australia's aspirations to middle power status. In contrast, Indonesia, hitherto once a major OPEC member has become a net importer of energy. The Study Group unfortunately could not get a grasp of Russia's position. The conventional assessment is that Russia could also emerge as an "energy power," but Russia's failure to participate in the Group's meetings left the Group with no understanding of how Russia perceives its position and impact on the reliability and affordability of its oil and gas supplies for its Asian neighbours.

The foregoing begs the question of how our position on the spectrum of supplier and consumer of energy and where we are on the runway to economic takeoff shapes our linkage of our energy supplies to our security. Underlying much of our Study Group discussions were a series of implicit and never explicitly articulated assumptions about the world around us. To the extent that most of us believed that our demand for fossil fuels will increase as we taxi to economic takeoff, and global reserves of fossil fuels are finite, then the policy instinct will be to move to secure and lock-up supplies. Further, if we perceive that the Sea Lanes of Communications along which all our oil moves, and our gas pipelines are vulnerable to a series of threats from piracy and terrorism to blockages by hostile groups or countries, then the security of our energy supplies becomes an existential threat. This matrix of implicit and deeply held geopolitical assumptions about our world then leads us to scan our horizons for weak signals of impending threats to either the supply or movement of our energy supplies and put in place contingency plans to pre-empt any threat to the supply and movement of our energy supplies.

However, a different series of implicit assumptions about our *globalised* world being more interdependent and cooperative than irreconcilable and combative could lead to a rather different linkage of energy supplies and security. Within this context, Study Group participants looked to learning from our European Union colleagues on how

Europe had managed to put in place a series of cooperative schemes and the infrastructure of electricity grids and gas pipelines for a more coordinated supply of their energy needs. Within the Asia Pacific both the APEC and ASEAN secretariats have been tasked to explore the prospects for laying down the infrastructure for a coordinated supply of our energy needs and the institutions needed to put in place such a coordinated, if not integrated supply of our energy. What are the prospects for Asia to learn from Europe and possibly cooperate for energy security?

Two different visions our world then drives our securitization of supplies of energy, especially fossil fuels. One is a rather traditional *geopolitical* vision of our world of nation states seeking to ensure their national interests by securing and locking-up supplies of energy. The other is a vision of a *globalised* and interdependent world that should be working for cooperative strategies to coordinate their energy needs. Further, a growing awareness of the impact of carbon emissions from our soaring energy consumption on our environment complexes this securitization of our energy needs. In the Royal Dutch Shell Company strategic planning, this is the "*scramble* scenario" versus the "*blueprint* scenario" of energy security.[2]

1.2 How is Supply of Energy a Security Issue? The Dimensions of Insecurity of Energy Supplies

How we disaggregate the supply of energy as a security issue is shaped in large part by why in the first instance energy supplies is a security issue that could become an existential threat. The current conventional wisdom is that our economic well-being and security is threatened if nation states cannot be assured of a *stable* supply of energy at an affordable price. Would policy options that lead to some kind of regional futures market for oil and natural gas and

---

2 http://www-static.shell.com/static/public/downloads/brochures/corporate_pkg/scenarios/shell_energy_ scenarios_2050.pdf

improvement to the efficiency of energy markets alleviate our insecurities of our energy supplies? However, if we are more concerned about the impact to our environment of carbon emissions from our increasing consumption of fossil fuels, then our disaggregating of energy supplies as a security issue will focus on human security and stress the search for *sustainable* alternative energy sources which are cleaner and more environmentally friendly. If on the contrary we believe that assuring our supply of energy and its transport is a more immediate and critical imperative for our economic development at this point of time than longer term issues of impact on the environment of our carbon emissions, then we will disaggregate our energy supplies insecurities to focus more on the formulation of policy options to *secure* and protect our energy supplies and its transportation. Much of the initial discussions of the Study Group focused on how we are disaggregating the insecurity of our energy supplies in the search for policy options to ensure the supplies of our energy needs.

For most of us the fundamental imperative is the risk of uncertain and potentially diminishing supplies of energy and threats to the energy distribution networks which challenges us. One category of policy options must therefore address the SECURITY of our energy supplies. A second dimension of linking our energy supplies to our security is the STABILITY of our energy supplies. The Study Group examined the relationship between supply and demand for energy and the policy issue of whether price volatility can be stabilized by policy options that strengthens regional cooperation and improves the efficiency of the energy market.

The Study Group also recognized that we are today going beyond issues of the SECURITY and STABILITY of our energy supplies to long term issues about the SUSTAINABILITY of our current patterns and trends of energy consumption. If, as we increasingly assess the trend and our pattern of energy consumption may be unacceptable, then what are the policy options for a more SUSTAINABLE energy future? As our Japanese colleague documented, Japan leads the drive for a more sustainable energy future through the more efficient use of available sources of energy. Other Study Group participants argued for development of alternative energy sources. Some participants thought the future lay in bio-fuels. Other participants thought that nuclear energy, once considered dangerous, has now become an acceptable risk.

Development of these three categories of concerns about the security of our energy supplies became a major focus of the Study Group's deliberations and policy recommendation. Much of the Study Group's discussions were structured around clarifying the threats to the SECURITY of our supplies of energy and the distribution networks and how to resolve these challenges and threats to the SECURITY of our energy supplies through policy options for a more STABLE and SUSTAINABLE energy future.

1.3 Generating Policy Options for a more Stable and Sustainable Energy Future

The Study Group brought together a wide variety of expertise to generate policy options for a more stable and sustainable energy future. This volume is an edition of some of the papers presented at the Study Group's meetings. I sensed that underlying much of the discussion and most of the papers is a tacit assumption that technology can improve the availability of fossil fuels; enhance the exploration of conventional fuel sources, improve the efficiency of our current use of energy or develop alternative energy sources. However, there was also an underlying uncertainty about the outcomes and viability of new technologies for development of bio-fuels and exploitation of oil-sands and oil-shale. The issue is not only one of the financial outlays for research and development into these technologies, but the more fundamental issue of the risk in relying on these new technologies. Unfortunately this issue of what is to be considered *acceptable risk* in depending upon technology to resolve our growing energy needs was not discussed by the Group? As with other issues of technology (for example, genetically modified food) is "acceptable risk" an issue of quantitative measurement of probability of success of the new technology, or is it a more qualitative perception of the uncertainty and therefore, fear of the new technology and its possible unanticipated consequences? Framed this way, the issue then becomes who decides what is *acceptable risk*? It is society who has to bear the consequences of possible failure of the technology, or the unintended effects of the technology? Or, is it governments who shape and regulate the criteria of what is *acceptable risk*? In the 1950s the issue of nuclear energy and its acceptability was the purview of technical experts and government regulators. But with public awareness of the potential dangers of nuclear energy from the 1970s onwards, the issue became an issue of governance; how do governments convince the public that nuclear energy is an *acceptable risk*? This area of risk in relying on a technoscience approach to security of our energy supplies is perhaps an area future CSCAP Study Groups may take up.

However, more participants at our Study Group were concerned about geopolitical risks which could threaten access to energy supplies. Some participants perceived the upgrading and modernization of navies in the region as a partial response to ensuring that access to energy supplies through the sea lanes remains unimpeded. China's concerns about the security of the Malacca Straits (and Hormuz Straits) through which its oil supplies flow and consequent intentions to develop a blue water navy to protect its interests were one focus of discussions, with one of our Chinese colleagues assuring us that this is a misreading of China's strategies. The possible threats to energy infrastructures – oil and gas pipelines, power stations (especially nuclear) and offshore oil platforms – were another focus of interest among participants and how to respond to any threat to these infrastructures.

In line with CSCAP's vision there was more discussion on how to reduce our insecurities about our supplies of energy and strengthen regional cooperation for a more accessible, affordable and acceptable supply of energy. Study Group participants debated the need for more transparent and efficient energy markets and in particular the case for a regional futures market for oil and natural gas. But Study Group participants also recognized that this advocacy of market mechanisms as a solution to a more stable delivery of regional energy resources is challenged by short-term market instability and therefore the need for some forms of market governance. Further, it appears that few governments are prepared to rely on market mechanisms entirely for a reliable, adequate and affordable supply of energy and continue to perceive energy supplies as a strategic resource which the state must intervene to protect. Despite these challenges to a more stable supply of our energy needs, the Study Group basically concluded that we must continue to work for more regional cooperation of our energy needs, rather than lapse into a more competitive world to control and confine energy supplies.

1.4 Pushing Policy Choices

The conventional textbook teaching of policy analysis is that the selection of a policy option is a rational choice of maximizing benefits. However, the uncertainties of an increasingly globalised world create more open and complex futures in which, as the *Shell energy Scenarios to 2050* stresses, "there are no ideal answers." The strategic planning of policy based on projecting a past trend into the future no longer holds when the present leads into multiple possible futures. Our geopolitical vision of the future of energy supplies leading us to attempt to lock up supply-side levers and unlock demand-side policies for economic growth is creating unintended consequences for our environment and leading us into new unplanned futures. But the alternative globalised future of an integrated Asian Energy Market the Study Group envisioned has been challenged by market failures and thumped by geopolitical imperatives to act unilaterally and compete for favourable terms of supply.

However the need for simplicity in policy analysis and recommendations lead members of the Study Group to confine their deliberations to the realm of our "Known Knowns" predictable world.

Within this predictable and ordered world the Policy Memorandum on Energy and Security we drafted attempted to first, make *sense* of the incoming data on our soaring energy needs on our security, second, *categorize* our responses as concern about the *Security* of our energy supplies, attempting to *Stabilize* our needs for energy, and plan for a more *Sustainable* energy future and third, *respond* on how to move ahead. Within this confines of how to respond within a predictable and ordered world, the Group responded by recommending better cooperation between energy suppliers and consumers across the region. Recognizing the challenges confronting the development of an Asian oil and gas market led the Group to recommend the need for industry and market reforms, more information sharing for greater transparency so as to enhance market stability and confidence building. Restated the Group's recommendations were improvements to what is considered "Best Practice."

In confining its deliberations to the realm of predictable "Known Knowns", the Group did not take up the challenge of attempting to evaluate the consequences of its proposed solutions. Thus the Group recommendation for a more *sustainable* energy future is to continue with the development of renewable forms of energy such as biofuels, solar, and hydroelectric energy and to harness them with the energy mix. This is improvement to what is currently "Best Practice." But is it also "Good Practice"? What are the consequences of the technologies we are recommending on our future? These are the "Known Unknown" outcomes and consequences of processing oil sands and shales or developing hydroelectric projects like the Greater Mekong River Project on our environment. What is the *risk* of these technologies and projects? Is it an *acceptable risk*? Perhaps another study Group could take up this challenge of analyzing and evaluating the consequences of proposed solutions to the security of our energy supplies today.

2

The Economics of Energy Security

YOUNGHO CHANG

Epigraph

Energy security can be defined as an adequate and reliable supply of energy at a reasonable price. Following this definition, the economics of energy security examines the economic consequences of volatile oil prices and the effectiveness of mitigation measures mainly for oil-importing countries. The stylized impacts of high oil prices are slowness in economic growth, a higher inflation and an increase in unemployment. Apart from the energy security for oil-importing countries, the energy security for oil-exporting countries in specific and depletable resource-based economies in general requires those economies to prepare for both the ultimate depletion of resources and the eventual loss of customers. A transition to a renewable capital-based economy is suggested as the solution for ensuring energy security.

2.1 Introduction

There are four broadly defined drivers for energy security: economics, politics, geopolitics and international relations. Economics is basically associated with market fundamentals such as imbalances between demand for and supply of energy that influence energy security, while national political agenda such as energy independence debates and fuel subsidy arguments alter perspectives of energy security beyond the jurisdiction of economics. When national political agenda is intertwined with geographical regions, it alters the ways and means of ensuring energy security and intensifies even security in a conventional sense. Iran's stance for a pro-nuclear energy policy conflicts with efforts of non-proliferation policy by western countries, and the drift between the two are diverging and is considered one of the main conflicting security issues. The European Union is in a serious dilemma between tapping more energy to African countries ignoring their undemocratic behaviour and regimes and promoting democracy in the continent by shunning energy from the African soil. Politics and market principles collide in the relationships between Russia and the EU in which the former uses energy as a way to influence relations within the EU while the latter asserts to adhere to market principles in determining energy supply. Finally, in international relations energy has been used as a way towards gearing up diplomatic gains. Venezuela has been providing oil to its neighbouring countries at prices far lower than the world price. The gains in international relations are achieved at the sizable economic losses and this also contributes to change the sphere of energy security arguments.

Among the four identified drivers, this study examines how the economic drivers have shaped the energy security and present policy recommendations that would help ensure energy security. This chapter is structured as follows: Section

2.2 shows how volatile oil prices have been over the years and investigates how these fluctuations have affected economic performances. It also examines what has attributed to those highly volatile movements of oil prices. Section 2.3 presents a scenario analysis as to what oil-exporting need to do ensure not only energy security but the sustainability of its economy as a long-term goal. Following the scenario analysis, verdicts on what would happen in the long-run are given in section 2.4. Section 2.5 concludes this study.

2.2 The Economics of Energy Security: Oil Price Fluctuations and the Economy

Historical oil price data shows that oil prices are inherently volatile and they go up and come down. Though a minor downturn in oil price movements have been shown, there has been a clear, steady and strong upward trend since 2007 until as recently as August 2008 shown below in various oil price paths.

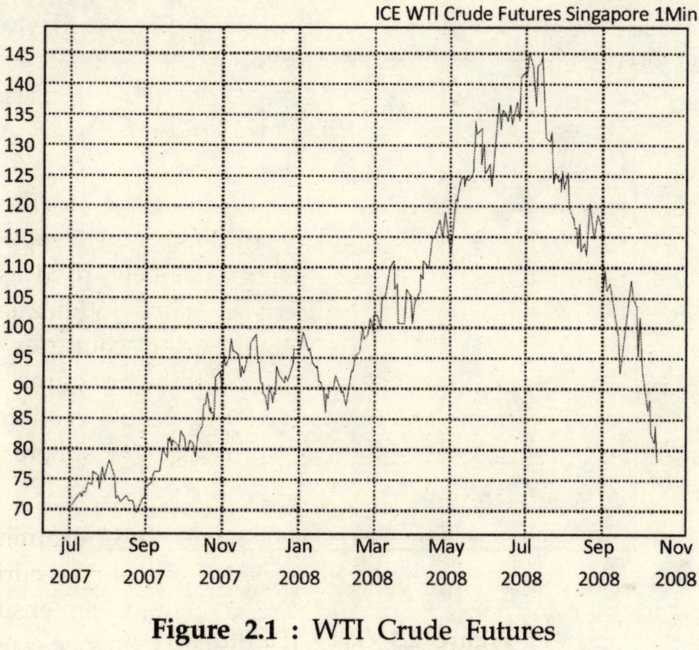

Figure 2.1 : WTI Crude Futures

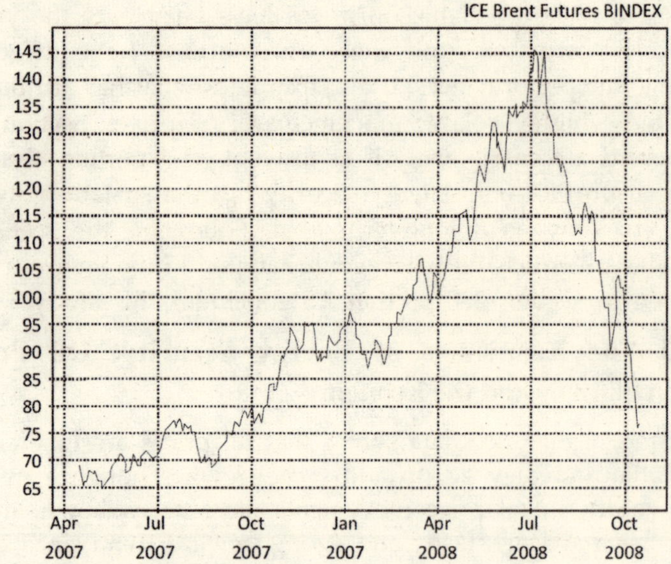

Figure 2.2 : Brent Futures

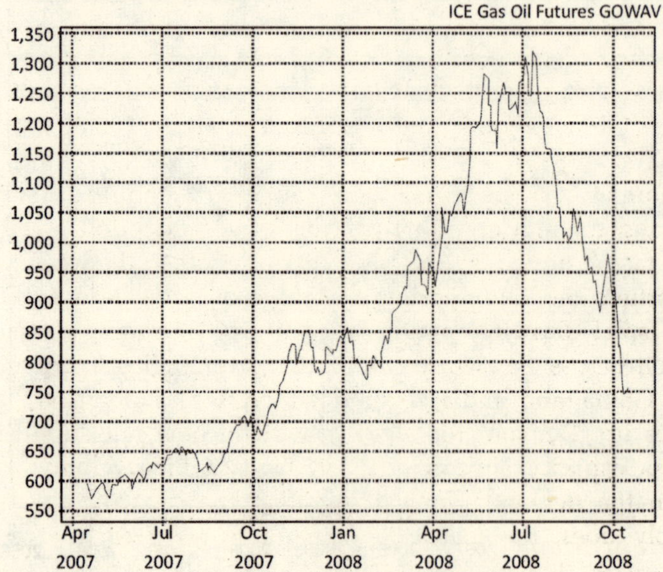

Figure 2.3 Gas Oil Futures

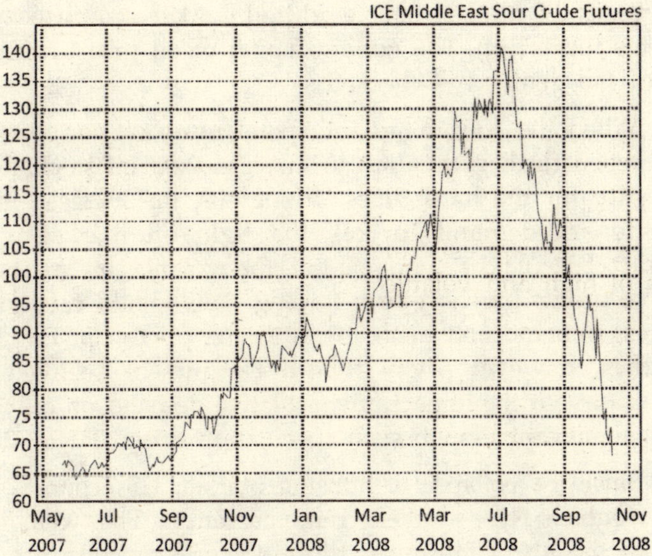

Figure 2.4 : Middle East Sour Crude Futures

Though current oil prices are hovering around \$50 per barrel, the price level in 2006, the recent crude awakening has revived the interests of what has caused the oil price close to \$150 per barrel. The crude awakening could be explained mainly by three factors (a) – steady and strong demand for oil from both developed and developing economies, (b) an increase in cautionary and speculative demand for oil, (c) a long-prevailing weak US dollar and a fear factor nested in the long-lasting conflicts between oil-exporting and oil-importing countries over the Middle East and Israel (Brown, Virmani and Alm, 2008). Strong demand for oil across the world, especially in emerging economies like China and India, is understood to have pushed oil prices up. Demand for oil rises with income but suppliers' excess capacity shrinks as they increase their supply. But when the demand grows faster than the capacity vis-à-vis supply does, the increased demand is not fully matched. The excess demand has to make the price to increase and a new equilibrium derived at a higher price. This in turn squeezes the already tight world oil market and push the oil prices further up. The upward spiral of oil prices continues until the demand is checked.

When the consumers anticipate future oil supply to be tightened further, they opt to increase their oil stockpiles to prepare for the hard times. Alongwith the increase in the cautionary demand for oil, the tight oil market would attract speculators who exploit the volatile oil market to make profits by short-term trading. This would cause more excess demand and hence push the oil prices up. Empirical studies, however, show that the argument seems to be plausible but the impact of speculative demand on oil prices is insignificant though such speculation exists (Helm, 2007).

Since the collapse of housing market, US economy was in trouble. This weakened its currency. The weakening dollar has also contributed to the increases in oil prices. As crude oil is traded in US dollar, the weaker US dollar gives oil exporting countries lower returns in the local currency. Hence those oil exporting countries opt to recover the possible losses by increasing the nominal prices of crude oil traded in the world oil market. (Now this trend has been reversed as US economy has become weaker and its impacts have spread over the global economy. Since the financial crisis in the world has deepened, the US dollar has become a bit stronger and oil prices are decreasing due to various causes including weaker US and the world economy.)

A fear factor due to geopolitical risks nested in oil exporting countries and neighbouring countries is considered to cause world oil prices up. For instance, tensions between Iran and Israel are expected to deepen and there are growing expectations that this will disrupt oil supply and increase the prices of crude oil. However, this is very elusive and hard to quantify its impact on oil prices.

After the Olympic in Beijing, the housing market in the US has collapsed and consequently it has caused the financial system in the US on the verge of bankruptcy. The financial crisis is sweeping not only the US but all markets in the world. Since the Olympic, oil prices have shown a clear downward trend among all of benchmark oil prices, namely West Texas Intermediate (WTI) Crude Futures, Brent Crude Futures and Middle East Sour Crude Futures. The decreasing oil prices, however, do not remove the negative consequences of volatile crude oil prices on an economy. Rather, the recent crude awakening has revived the interests of evaluating the economic consequences of high and volatile oil prices along with what has caused the awakening.

There are four broadly defined drivers for energy security such as economic, political, geopolitical and international relations. Apart from these drivers of energy security, the energy security can be more specifically defined as "an adequate and reliable supply of energy at a reasonable price" (Bielecki, 2002). The economics literature on the impact of oil price fluctuations on an economy covers the economic consequences of volatile (and mainly increasing) oil prices for oil-importing countries and the ways of mitigating the impacts. The path that volatile oil prices incur costs on oil-importing countries is through the production and consumption framework of a modern economy where oil is an input for production along with capital and labour and a final good for consumption. A production function with energy or oil as an input factor is expressed as follows:

$$Q = Q(K, L, E),$$

where

Q is the output,

K is the capital,

L is the labour,

E is the energy and $Q(\bullet)$ is the production technology.

With increasing oil prices, an economy that uses oil as an input faces basically two options. One is sustaining the level of oil consumption even under higher oil prices and the other is reducing oil input for its production process. The former will leave less resource or income available for the economy to hire capital and labour and results in lowering output. The latter will also give less output as lower amount of energy enters into the production process assuming capital and labour are hired at the same level.

The same goes for consumers. Sustaining the same level of fuel consumption will leave the consumers with less income available for other expenses and reduce their utility derived from the consumption. Reducing fuel consumption, every other thing remains constant, will lower the consumers' utility.

There are several ways of diminishing the impacts of high oil prices on an economy: Storing petroleum for a precautionary purpose, hedging short-term price risks, using portfolios connecting asset values to energy prices, investing in production technology and hence increasing energy efficiency. There are policy measures such as long-term oil import restrictions through imposing quotas or tariffs, imposing energy taxes, increasing domestic supply by altering rules and regulations limiting domestic supply, accumulating and releasing oil stockpiles and coordinating policies among oil-importing countries.

Even under these measures and policies, an oil price shock is considered a "classical supply shock" and the economic impacts of high oil prices are slow economic growth, high inflation and high unemployment. In the past, this classical definition was well suited with the economic consequences of high oil prices. High oil prices had caused severe recessions. However, recent surge in oil prices have not brought impacts as severe as the past incidences did. There are still negative impacts but the stylized negative causation is weakening. The weakening relationship is expected to continue.

Why such digression has occurred has been studied. Empirical evidence of the negative relationship is mixed and various reasons for the weakening are suggested. First, more stable aggregate demand absorbs the impacts of high cost due to surging oil prices. Second, the level of energy intensity across the world has decreased, so the economy is less vulnerable to oil price surge. Third, a greater flexibility is in the economy and hence it is more resilient to a shock. Fourth, governments have better monetary policy and know how to react to oil shocks unlike in the 70s and 80s. Fifth, the recent oil price shock is a demand shock rather than a supply shock, and it is slightly different from being a "classical supply shock" (Brown and Yucel, 2003). The negative causation is expected to weaken further in the future.

How an economy responses to high oil prices could be summarized in two ways — short-term and long-term. In the short-term, reducing oil uses or sustaining the same level of oil use and bear the full costs of high oil prices are the only viable options. In the long-term, however, an economy can substitute alternative fuels for oil and recover to the pre-shock level. It could even achieve a higher level of economic growth. What had happened during and after two oil shocks showed huge improvements in energy efficiency across the economy, economywise energy conservation efforts even after oil price returned to lower level. They had also witnessed developments of new sources of energy and technologies such as secondary fuels like CTL and unconventional fossil fuels. These new energy sources replaced oil mainly in power generations. Some "alternative" energy could become "energy" one day.

The underlying arguments present how high oil prices induced and encouraged technology developments — an ultimate solution for solving energy crisis and the eventual depletion of conventional energy sources. Even oil prices have gone down in the late 1980s and the 1990s, the world has witnessed that the substitution of oil for alternatives keeps occurring in many areas of an economy, efforts to improve energy efficiency and energy conservation still continue. The demand for oil in terms of the unit of oil per output will decrease further. And the level of energy intensity in terms of the unit of energy requirements per

GDP is decreasing over time. In sum, the share of oil in the world energy consumption keeps decreasing in the future. The ensuing confinement of oil into a very indispensable demand will elongate the lifespan of oil even farther than the current reserve/production ratio envisages.

2.3 Energy Security for Oil-Exporting Countries: A Scenario Analysis

High oil prices eventually have made the economy improve energy efficiency, conserve energy, help develop new technologies and lead the economy use less oil and eventually switch to a new and abundant energy source. In this regard, high oil prices seem to be a blessing disguised in a disaster. What is then a worst scenario for oil-exporting countries between the ultimate depletion of oil and the ultimate loss of consumers due to transition to a backstop technology? The question is which one is most likely to occur. The two scenarios are as follows:

Scenario A: The ultimate depletion of oil reserves

Scenario B: The ultimate loss of customers

The scenario A states that oil reserves will deplete geologically as the reserves are finite while scenario B states that the oil reserves could reach an economic depletion point, which is earlier than the geological one, though the resources are still technologically extractable. When a country exhausts its oil reserves, there will not be further income stream if it does not have other capital for producing goods and services. The same thing will happen if the country does not have any customers who are willing to buy its produce and the sale of the produce is its only (or major) income source. The ultimate loss of customers could happen if its prices are higher than the prices of other suppliers and other resources that can replace its resource.

A Saudi proverb says "My father rode a camel. I drive a car. My son flies a jet airplane. His son will ride a camel."

This reflects a mentality of laymen at an oil-exporting country. Oil is one of the typical depletable resources. When it is extracted and sold, it brings revenues to the country. The revenues can be used for accumulating man-made capital for reproduction and be consumed away by lifting their vanity consumption from riding a car to flying a jet airplane. When a depletable resource-based economy does not accumulate enough capital for future production, income in the future will not be flowing nor it will be enough for sustaining the level of consumption that its earlier generations indulge.

A former Saudi Arabia oil minister also warned the oil-exporting countries may lose their customers before they deplete the resource they have. Altogether, these emphasize that the necessity of transforming a depletable capital-based economy to a rzzzzenewable-based economy. Oil-dependent economy need to be prepared for both scenarios to make the economy at least weakly sustainable in which a constant level of consumption vis-à-vis well-being is sustained so that there is no degradation of living.

2.4 Energy Security for Non-Oil-Exporting Countries

The underlying imperative of switching a depletable resource-based economy to a renewable capital-based economy does not apply to only oil-exporting countries. The disastrous case in the Aral Sea exemplifies this situation in which a failure of moving its economy towards a renewable capital-based one brings only a regrettable state. The Aral Sea is located in Uzbekistan and Kazakhstan and was the fourth largest in the world in the 1960s. Over-irrigation caused salinization of the Aral Sea reducing it to the eight largest in the world now. A large ship anchored in the shore of the Aral Sea, which is called as a ship "cemetery," only tells the productive old days.

A more worrying case could be the situation facing Nauru, a small island with land area of 21 km^2 in the Pacific

Ocean, whose sole source for revenue is exporting phosphates, a feedstock for fertilizer. Nauru is abundant in phosphates, but the problem is it is part of their land on which Nauruan inhibits. It could meet its revenue requirements by selling phosphates. However, more selling of phosphates can be only achieved by reducing its inhabitable land. The more phosphates are exported, the less land for inhabitation remains. Here is a dilemma for the authorities to figure out how to replete the depleted resource. Nauru should thrive in a solution with which it can sustain its existence at the location where it is now or elsewhere. Actually, Nauru invested the proceeds from selling phosphates into a real estate business in Australia, Hawaii, Guam, Fiji and New Zealand and funded millions in a trust fund. But the worldwide collapse in real estate market ignited by the end of Japanese's panic buying of real estate in Honolulu gave Nauru poor returns. Along with the poor returns from those investments, corruption and the Asian financial crisis made the Nauru's trust fund bankrupt. Nauru's trial is considered a failure.

Unlike the Aral Sea and Nauru, the United Arab Emirates (UAE) could present a successful case of switching a depletable resource-based economy to a renewable capital-based economy by diversifying its economy into non-resource based economy. When an economy can sustain its consumption level over time, it can be considered a weakly-sustainable economy following the definition of weak sustainability.[1] Intense non-oil capital investments such as harbours, airports and other infrastructure started in the 1960s and oil exports contribute to 9 per cent of its GDP in 2003, which is down from over 50 per cent in 1975. It has achieved compound growth rate of 8 per cent per annum for the past decade. Whether the UAE can present a workable example for other depletable capital-based economy remains to be seen, but the current affluence in the UAE is

1 For the definition of weak sustainability, see *Hartwick* (1977).

considered a success and as an example for other economies to adopt its (UAE) strategy for sustaining their economies.

2.5 Upshot

Slow economic growth, spiralling inflation, unemployment etc are concomitants of an economy burdened to bear the costs of high oil prices. This is a precarious situation which can be evaded by putting oil to use for indispensable purposes. At the same time, high oil prices would be motivating factor for exploration and production (E&P) of indigenous oil and the developments of new sources of energy and technologies.

In the long-run, oil will be spared for very specific and non-substitutable energy demand and hence the availability of oil will be extended compared to the situation where oil is used for all energy demand categories. High oil prices will accelerate the developments of alternative fuels or backstop technologies such as portable PV, fuel cells or hydrogen. The transition towards a renewable energy-based economy would occur more rapidly. This way the market will have benefit of availability of abundant supply of energy at a reasonable and affordable price.

Such measures will not only contain the volatile oil prices, but also minimize the magnitude of the consequences thereby helping the economy to become less vulnerable to volatile oil prices. The right oil prices convey correct signals to both producers and consumers making new energy sources economically more competitive and commercially viable. This eventually makes alternative an energy of the future. Simultaneously, when oil—or depletable resource—based economy makes a gradual and successful transition to a renewable capital-based one, the economy will become at somewhat sustainable and making a steady income-flow. Such a scenario will ensure a reliable supply of energy at a reasonable price.

Bibliographical References

1. Adelman, M. A., "World Oil Production and Prices 1947–2000," *Quarterly Review of Economics and Finance*, 42: 169–191 (2002).
2. Barton, Barry, Catherine Redgwell, Anita Rønne, and Donald Zillman (eds.), *Energy Security: Managing Risk in a Dynamic Legal and Regulatory Economics*, Oxford University Press, 2004.
3. Bentley, R. W., "Global Oil and Gas Depletion: An Overview," *Energy Policy*, 30: 189–205 (2002).
4. Bielecki, B., "Energy Security: Is the Wolf at the Door?" *Quarterly Review of Economics and Finance*, 42: 235–250 (2002).
5. Bohi, Douglas R. and Michael A. Toman, *The Economics of Energy Security*. Kluwer Academic Publishers, 1996.
6. Brown, Stephen P.A. and Mine K. Yucel, "Business Cycles: The Role of Energy Prices," *Research Department Working Paper* 0304, Federal Reserve Bank of Dallas (2003)
7. Brown, Stephen P.A., Raghav Virmani and Richard Alm, "Crude Awakening: Behind the Surge in Oil Prices," *Economic Letter: Insights from the Federal Reserve Bank of Dallas*, Vol. 3, No. 5 (2008)
8. Chang, Youngho and Jian Liang Lee, "Electricity Market Deregulation and Energy Security: A Study of the UK and Singapore Electricity Markets," *International Journal of Global Energy Issues*, 29(1/2): 109–132 (2008)
9. Chang, Youngho and Jiayun Yong, "Differing Perspectives of Major Oil Firms on Future Energy Developments: An Illustrative Framework," *Energy Policy*, 35: 5466–5480 (2007)
10. Griffin, James M., "OPEC Behavior: A Test of Alternative Hypotheses," *American Economic Review*, 75(5): 954–963 (1985)
11. Hartwick, John M., "Intergenerational Equity and the Investing of Rents from Exhaustible Resources," *American Economic Review*, Vol. 67, No. 5, 972-974 (1977)

12. Helm, Dieter (ed.), *The New Energy Paradigm*, Oxford University Press, 2007.

13. Kalicki, Jan H. and David L. Goldwyn (eds.), *Energy & Security: Toward a New Foreign Policy Strategy*, Woodrow Wilson Center Press, Washington, D.C., 2005

14. Kneese, Allen V. and James L. Sweeney (eds.), *Handbook of Natural Resource and Energy Economics*, Volume III, North-Holland, 1993 (Chapter 25 only).

15. Kohl, Wilfred L., "OPEC Behavior, 1998–2001," *Quarterly Review of Economics and Finance*, 42: 209 – 233 (2002).

16. Kumar, Nagesh, K. Kesavapany and Yao Chaocheng, *Asia's New Regionalism and Global Role: Agenda for the East Asia Summit*, Research and Information System for Developing Countries (RIS), New Delhi and Institute of Southeast Asian Studies (ISEAS), Singapore, 2008

17. Mabro, Robert (ed.), *Oil in the* 21st *Century: Issues, Challenges and Opportunities*, Oxford University Press, 2006.

18. Mitchell, John V., "A New Political Economy of Oil," *Quarterly Review of Economics and Finance*, 42: 251–272 (2002).

19. Nordhaus, William D., *The Efficient Use of Energy Resources*, Yale University Press, 1979

20. Noreng, Øystein, *Crude Power: Politics and the Oil Market*, L. B. Tauris, 2002.

21. Wirl, Franz, "Why Do Oil Prices Jump (or Fall)?' *Energy Policy*, 36: 1029–1043 (2008)

3

An Assessment on Energy Infrastructure Security

DR. CHUNG-YOUNG CHANG

3.1 Background

Since the end of the Cold War, various forms of "non-traditional security threats, both man-made and natural" have come to the forefront, Critical national infrastructure (CNI) has been widely regarded as the lifeblood of any country (RUSI (UK), 2008). The issue of critical national infrastructure protection (CNIP) has thus been commonly deemed as a key public policy, and a major issue in the agenda of national security policy for governments in the contemporary threat scenario (Conference Report, 2006).

Among the major sectors of CNI and in the light of national practices across the world, Energy Infrastructure Security (EIS) is receiving greater strategic and security attention at national, regional and global levels. As major countries start to place EIS at the heart of CNIP with national efforts, the importance and prominence of EIS is even more highlighted in the wake of several man-made or natural disasters or just system breakdowns, including terrorist attack of 2002 against oil tank *Limburg* at sea, the power outage of 2003 in eastern Canada and US, and devastating effects of a series of natural disasters such as tsunami, earthquake and storm in the past five years.

As per the prevailing trend the issue of EIS will continue to be in the center of national policy and will be an essential part of energy security. This article intends to explore and assess the security of energy infrastructure. It will begin by outlining essence of energy infrastructure security from the perspective of the process of energy production, transportation, storage and distribution. It will continue to analyze emerging threats or risk factors to the security of energy infrastructure and assess various dimensions of vulnerability of EIS. The main purpose of this article is to conduct a threat analysis and security assessment so as to understand better what challenges we are facing and what solutions may be required.

3.2 Essences of Energy Infrastructure Security

While energy security is most often related to growing demand and competition for energy, increasing dependence on energy imports, high and volatile oil prices, the need for promoting a clean environment and improving energy efficiency, conservation and diversity, it is also seriously concerned with various threats of disruption in energy supply and the vulnerability of critical energy infrastructure security. It is beyond doubt that the security of energy infrastructure is one of the most essential safeguards that will provide an uninterrupted and sustainable supply of energy (Sinyugin, Oleg A, 2006).

In fact, the issue of EIS has often been raised not only in energy policy of many countries, but also via a number of regional and global efforts. For instance, energy security in general and EIS in particular have been the main theme for annual APEC Energy Ministerial Meeting and ASEAN Ministers on Energy Meeting (AMEM). In addition, G8 Summit, UN meetings and other major international forum have also focussed on the issue of energy security in the past decade.

In view of the nature and practices in EIS that transcends ministerial responsibilities of a single country and operates across national boundaries, to secure energy infrastructure will require all relevant state and non-state stakeholders in the supply chain from energy production and transit countries to the consumption markets to work together. As has been advocated, EIS needs to employ "a holistic approach that looks at ends, ways and means to detect and explore energy resources and to refine, store, transport and distribute the relevant products" (Forster, Karina and Heiko Borchert, 2007). It is important to note that EIS will not be possible without a network of national and international governance that stresses transnational cooperation involving both public and private sectors (US Department of State, 2008 and Natural Resources Canada, 2006).

The primary task of EIS is to safeguard the physical safety and security of tangible properties of energy supply chain such as drilling facilities, refineries, pipelines, oil tanks, storages and control centers. In addition, the security of information and communication technology serving the purpose of control and command in energy supply is also crucial to the protection of EIS. Moreover, natural disasters of various kinds such as severe earthquakes or storms and industrial accidents caused by human negligence and deliberate attacks also pose great risks to EIS (Smallwood, Joseph, 2005).

It is especially important to note that the security of world's energy infrastructure is interdependent since no country can be totally immune from man-made or natural disasters against the security of energy infrastructure. It will require a holistic approach in promoting energy cooperation in various forms and at different levels to better safeguard EIS.

3.3 Threats to Energy Infrastructure Security

While major risks to energy security may include, as identified by a Japanese Energy Security Study Group in 2006, political conditions in energy producing countries/ areas such as the Middle East; terrorist attacks, natural disasters, and industrial accidents; reduction in upstream investment in supplier nations; and trend of rising demands for energy from countries such as China and India.

According to a report released by CRS in 2003, energy supply facilities, such as oil and gas pipelines, have often been a favoured target of terrorist attacks. For example, armed rebels in Colombia have bombed Occidental Petroleum's Caño Limón pipeline nearly 950 times since 1986, shutting it for months at a time and costing Colombian government some US $2.5 billion in lost revenue. In particular, one attack in 1998 caused a fire that killed and injured over 100 people. Another well-known case was in UK where London police foiled a plot by the IRA to bomb gas pipelines and other utilities across the city with 36 explosive devices in 1996. Oil and gas pipelines in Nigeria, Pakistan, Sudan, Myanmar and Iraq have also been attacked in the last five years. In Saudi Arabia, a planned pipeline attack by al-Qaeda sympathizers at the country's main oil terminal was thwarted in 2002. In October 2002, a French oil tank *Limburg* was attacked and caught fire resulting in spillage of about 90,000 barrels of oil into the Gulf of Aden. One crewman was killed in that incident and the cost of repairs amounted to US $45 million.

The Liquefied Natural Gas (LNG) tankers that play a key role in world energy supply chain (M.Flynn, Aroan and Paul W. Parfomak, 2004) deserve special attention. As of 2005, there were 176 LNG tankers in service and another 111 tankers on order around the world. In addition, there are at least 40 LNG marine terminals and 150 peak-shaving plants worldwide. However, since 1959, there has been no serious LNG accident at sea or in port, a favourable safety record except for the 1944 Cleveland fire. Nevertheless, given the nature of the LNG shipments, concern for the insecurity is quite legitimate: first, LNG is highly visible, easily identifiable, inherently volatile and stored in large quantity; second, LNG tankers, land based facilities and computer control systems are vulnerable to terrorist attacks or cyber-attacks; and finally, disruption of LNG shipping or storages poses additional "downstream" risks.

Moreover, as an LNG assessment report released by Sandia National Laboratories in December 2004 indicated that "an intentional LNG spill and resulting fire could cause major injuries to people and significant damage to structures within approximately 500 meters (0.3 mile) of the spillage site, more moderate injuries and structural damage upto 1,600 meters (1.0 mile) from the spillage site, with feeble collateral damages to 2,500 meters (1.5 miles). Another report released by Lloyd's Register in 2002 also pointed out that a deliberate attack (a hand-held missile attack and a bomb attack from a small boat) on an LNG carrier can result in a threat to both the ship, its crew and members of the public. It is still very difficult to assert definitely how dangerous a real attack would be, but the potential consequences of a terrorist incident against LNG or an LNG industrial accident deserves careful and serious attention.

To sum up, deliberate sabotage, or terrorist attacks, against energy infrastructure are widely regarded as the most dangerous sources of threats to EIS. Such attacks may take place at land or in sea and will raise the difficulties and costs in safeguarding EIS.

3.4 Vulnerabilities of Energy Infrastructure Security

Apart from the threats that endanger EIS as mentioned above, the security of energy infrastructure also needs to deal with the issues of the vulnerabilities that could place the normal supply of energy at high risks. In fact, looking for ways and means to reduce the vulnerabilities of EIS with an aim for sustaining or assuring energy supply to the importing countries has been one of the focal points of the regional and global security fora.

The vulnerabilities of EIS often stem from the predisposed weakness of the systems and the inadequacy of preparedness and management in response to emergencies. These may range from the impact of natural disasters, human errors and industrial accidents on the chain of energy supply to the lack of industrial investment, management and technology to improve or maintain the safety and security of the whole process of energy supply.

In August 2003, a massive power outage incident occurred in east coast of the US and eastern Canada. An estimated 10 million people in the province of Ontario (about 1/3 of the population of Canada) and 40 million people in eight US states (about 1/7 of the population of the US) were affected. The outage-related financial losses were estimated at US $6 billion. In December 2005, a major fire broke out in Hertfordshire Oil Storage Terminal (Bucefield Depot). The Terminal was the fifth largest oil-products storage depot in the UK accounting for about five per cent of UK oil storage capacity. It was a major hub on the UK's oil pipeline network (UKOP) with pipelines to Homberside and Mereyside and an important fuel source to the British aviation industry.

While the vulnerabilities of EIS are hard to rectify, the impact of an energy infrastructure emergency accident can be alleviated with the function of 'consequence management'. Moreover, cooperation between governments is also crucial in constructing a network of security safeguards for the security of energy infrastructure.

3.5 Challenges Ahead and Solutions Required

Energy security is critical to economic growth, military defence, social development, poverty reduction, national security and environmental security. Regional or even global energy infrastructure security cooperation is important to guarantee this security particularly in respect of as a guarantee-cross-border gas pipelines, local gas distribution systems, electricity generation units and transmission networks. However, there remain some challenges ahead (Asia Pacific Energy Research Center, 2000).

First, in addition to the factors of differing political regimes and legal systems that constitute a difficulty in the way of energy cooperation, tensions in the Middle East and Korean Peninsula, territorial disputes and other potential crises in East Asia may hinder cooperative relations. Unless the political situations in the region were to stabilise, cooperation on energy development or infrastructure security would be almost next to impossible (Chanlett-Avery, Emma, 2005).

Second, due to the lack of energy infrastructure construction and maintenance in the past years, huge long-term capital investment to finance the infrastructure projects is utmost needed. However, as development funds are limited, competition for funds required for investment in energy projects across the world may increase tensions rather than enhance cooperation. The gap between the more developed countries and the less developed ones will further increase as new energy projects will more likely be located in rich and strong nations (Asia Pacific Energy Research Center, 2004).

Third, apart from technical difficulties in energy development projects, social resistance and concern for environmental protection may constitute other major obstacles. Tensions or conflicts could become worse if political, social or ideological issues were to be involved. In fact, some energy infrastructure projects were suspended or halted as a result of strong protest of local or tribal community.

Fourth, it should be noted that uncertainty in political arena, financial instability and lack of sufficient legal and regulatory regime may inhibit foreign investment or pose substantial investment risks. Energy development projects, such as oilfields or coal mines, are often located in the countries that are vulnerable to foreign pressures and do not possess adequate resources for nation-building and sustainable development (Zhang, ZhongXiang and Won-Cheol Yun, 2005).

Finally, in recent years, it is often observed that power struggle between central and local governments and nationalistic assertion of ethnic minorities for charging resource development may be hurdles in the development of indigent energy infrastructure projects. The contention over energy infrastructure construction will be getting worse if political organizations or interest groups exercise their power of influence.

As the St. Petersburg Plan of Action of the 2006 Global Energy Security indicated, the following issues in securing critical energy infrastructure need to be addressed:

1. Defining and prioritizing the most important vulnerabilities among energy infrastructure sites, and share methodologies for assessing and mitigating them;
2. Assessing potential risks of terrorist attacks;
3. Developing a compendium of effective security response best practices across all energy sectors within different countries;
4. Developing, implementing, and providing to other countries a checklist for the physical security of critical energy infrastructure;
5. Encouraging international cooperation on R&D for technologies to enhance critical infrastructure protection;
6. Establishing points of contact for coordination of technical assistance in this area;
7. To advocate the adoption of export controls on radioactive sources and new initiatives to prevent terrorists' access to radioactive sources.
8. Finally, it also calls upon governments to fully implement the International Ships and Ports Facility

Security Code and encourage attention to the management of maritime security.

As the Plan of Action 2006 describes, a roadmap for the regional cooperation on energy infrastructure security may be outlined as follows:

1. Promoting cooperative relations and joint projects via regional institutional bodies, e.g. ASEAN(+3), EAS, and APEC. All relevant stakeholders, including energy production, transit and consumption countries, need to be brought together to engage in consultative process for solution;[1]
2. Raising awareness of mutual dependence and win-win relations and facilitating a cooperative network of public-private partnership, initiating forum for dialogue between government and business community;
3. Ensuring safe passage through the Strait of Malacca and South China Sea via regional framework of cooperation and arrangements for maritime security and emergency preparedness and response;
4. Facilitating information exchange and data sharing, including best practices and knowledge of research, via an institutional mechanism among all stakeholders, as one step of consensus and confidence building in forging regional cooperation;
5. Creating or strengthening institutionalized regional arrangements for multilateral energy cooperation including Energy Charter Treaty process based on principles of market economy, mutual assistance,

---

[1] *See*, "Energizing ASEAN to Power a Dynamic Asia," *Joint Ministerial Statement of the 25th ASEAN Ministers on Energy Meeting (AMEM)*, Singapore, 23 August 2007; *Joint Ministerial Statement of 4th ASEAN+3 (China, Japan and Korea) Ministers on Energy Meetings*, Singapore, 23 August 2007; and *Joint Ministerial Statement of the first EAS Energy Ministers Meeting*, Singapore, 23 August 2007.

public-private partnership and non-discrimination, toward an 'energy cooperation community' to deal with infrastructure financing, investment protection, dispute settlement, tax and tariff regarding energy cooperation;

6. Encouraging domestic capital investment for energy infrastructure, foreign direct investment, cooperation among countries and alternative approaches to infrastructure development and planning, with clear energy policies, market incentives, risk management, good governance and effective regulatory and institutional frameworks (US Department of Energy, 2002); and
7. Securing strong political and economic commitment of all stakeholder countries to initiate, among others, market restructuring or financial reform, with a common vision of energy security and a strategic plan on infrastructure cooperation.

3.6 Conclusion

As energy security has become more important in the agenda of national security policy, the security of energy infrastructure has become even more prominent. Regional and global energy security cooperation will become even more crucial as the threat posed by both man-made and natural disasters are on the rise. In fact, as the process of energy supply, including production, transportation and distribution, operates across national boundaries and consists of a number of complex components that are both essential and vulnerable, it will require cooperation at national, regional and even global levels to safeguard the security of energy infrastructure.

Bibliographical References

RUSI (UK), 4th *Annual Science and Technology for Homeland Security and Resilience Conference*, London, UK, June 25, 2008.

Conference Report, *IDSA-PRIO International Conference on the Geopolitics of Energy Security: the Rise of Asia*, New Delhi, India, 15-16 December 2006.

Sinyugin, Oleg A. *New Energy Infrastructure Development in Asia-Pacific Region*, Asia Pacific Energy Research Center, Japan, 2006.

Forster, Karina and Heiko Borchert, "Energy Infrastructure Security: Time For A Networked Public-Private Governance Approach," *Middle East Economic Survey*, May 2007.

US Department of State, Protecting Critical Physical Infrastructure, http://www.state.gov/t/pm/ppa/icipt/wci/, visited on 11 March 2008; and Natural Resources Canada, *Energy Infrastructure Protection Division (EIPD)-Formative Evaluation*, 29 September 2006.

Smallwood, Joseph, *The European Approach to Critical Energy Infrastructure Protection*, Security of Energy Facilities and Infrastructure, EAPC/PfP Workshop, Zurich, 23 September 2005.

Interim Report, *Energy Security Study Group*, Natural Resources and Energy Agency of Japan, June 2006.

M. Flynn Aaron and Paul W. Parfomak "Liquefied Natural Gas (LNG) Import Terminals: Siting, Safety and Regulation," *CRS Report for Congress, RL32205*, released on May 27, 2004.

Asia Pacific Energy Research Center, *Power Interconnection in the APEC Region*, Tokyo, March 2000.

Chanlett-Avery, Emma, *Rising Energy Competition and Energy Security in Northeast Asia: Issues for US Policy*, CRS Report for Congress, 9 February 2005.

Asia Pacific Energy Research Center, *Electric Power Grid Interconnections in the APEC Region*, 2004.

Zhang, ZhongXiang and Won-Cheol Yun, "Electric Power Grid Interconnection in Northeast Asia," *Working Papers No. 63*, East-West Center, March 2005.

US Department of Energy, *Energy Infrastructure Risk Management Checklists for Small and Medium Sized Energy Facilities*, 19 August 2002.

4

Energy and the Global Political Scenario

TALMIZ AHMAD

The events of September 11 have focused international attention on West Asia and engendered deep-seated concerns over energy insecurity considering that the five Gulf countries have 65 per cent of the world's oil resources. Soon after 9/11, certain American political leaders had vocally highlighted threats to US interests on account of its dependence on Middle East oil (Shelley, Toby, 2005).

Professor Øystein Noreng believes that the United States has embarked on a strategy of building a new empire in which the "control of the Middle East is a prerequisite, Iraq is a cornerstone and Iran remains the major obstacle" (Noreng, Øystein, 2006). The bloody and sustained insurgency in Iraq, the heightened confrontation with Iran and continuing violence in Palestine and Lebanon paint the picture of a West Asia mired in insecurity and violence and a breeding ground for Islamic extremists. This bleak situation has led commentators to speculate about long-term US plans for the region and the extent to which they would require modifications due to developments in Iraq.

There is consensus among observers that the neo-conservative pre-war gameplan of using a pro-American Iraq as the base to support long-term US plans to dominate West Asia politically and militarily, and pursue policies to reform and, if necessary, to remap the region to suit Washington's interests, seem to have failed. Most commentators now fear that Iraq faces the real prospect of civil war, which could encompass the entire region as Iraq's neighbours rally around their sectarian allies, even as Turkey flexes its military muscle to contain Kurdish aspirations for independence. Such a scenario would lead to prolonged instability in a region central to the global oil economy.

US "empire-building" policies in Iraq and attempts to dominate West Asia strategically are being played out in a global environment that is in considerable flux, with the principal players pursuing a number of regional initiatives in support of their strategic interests, largely tied to energy security considerations. The Indian strategic affairs commentator, Brahma Chellaney, has pointed out that a qualitative reordering of power (is) underway, and that the shifts in international power – most conspicuous in Asia – are occurring due to a factor unique to the modern world: rapid economic growth. The central characteristic of these shifts in international power is the fact that all important players, including China, are manoeuvring for geopolitical advantage through new equations and initiatives.

The trilateral Russia–China–India dialogue, examined above, is an attempt by the principal players in Asia to identify and pursue matters that promote their strategic, primarily energy-related interests. In an attempt to counter this, the United States is seeking to engage India in a strong strategic embrace based on the India–US Nuclear Agreement as also by involving it in the new "Quadrilateral Initiative" made up of the US, Japan, Australia and India. This group had its first meeting at the end of May 2007 on the margins of the ASEAN Regional Forum [ARF] meeting in Manila. This was preceded by a US–India naval exercise at Okinawa, followed by a Japan–US–India exercise. In between, India dispatched some of its ships for a friendly exercise with China (Chellaney, Brahma, 2007).

A number of interests and alliances are being pursued in Asia at present, indicating that, for the moment, no security architecture has emerged that is exclusive and actively hostile to another country or group. For instance, each member of the Quadrilateral Initiative has substantial economic and political links with China. While the United States is actively wooing India as an ally (on par with Japan and Australia), it is simultaneously building up political and economic relations with China and continues to provide military, political and economic support to Pakistan.

Given the multiplicity of groups and the multiple interests being pursued by them, Chellaney has suggested that it would be in India's interest to participate in a number of different triangular initiatives such as those that would bring Russia, India and Japan together, as also Japan, China and India, which, taken together, would encourage strategic transparency and understanding (Chellaney, Brahma, 2007). In this context, it is interesting to note that the distinguished RoK scholar and Member of Parliament, Chung Duck-Koo, has advocated a "new Triangular Partnership" embracing Northeast Asia, ASEAN and Southwest Asia (=South Asia). (Duck-Koo, Chung, 2006). In support of this proposal, he has noted three distinct areas of strength of these partners: Northeast Asia's manufacturing sector, ASEAN's natural resources and India's services and IT technology. He sees these capacities as complementary, and believes that mutual cooperation would, in due course, lead the partner-countries to achieve "similar level of economic development." The first step in the realization of this triangular cooperation, according to Chung, is the pursuit of bilateral engagements in trade, investment, development assistance as well as enhanced diplomatic ties. Sino-Indian relations, which constitute the centerpiece of the strategic jostling underway in Asia at present, may be analyzed in this broad strategic context.

4.1 India and China in the Global Scenario

Based on existing trends, China and India are expected to emerge as the new major world powers by 2020. According to some studies, China, by 2020, will have a population of 1.4 billion, the second largest GDP in dollar terms (US$7 trillion dollars) after the United States (US$17 trillion), and the largest economy in purchasing power parity terms (US$29.6 trillion), followed by the United States (US$28.8 trillion). Its demand for oil would be almost equal to that of the United States, while its defense expenditure would amount to US$150 billion in 2020 assuming a medium rate of growth, as against US$439 billion proposed by President Bush for the fiscal year 2007 (Hussain, Javid).

The economic gap between China and the United States is already shrinking gradually. In 1979, the year Deng Xiaoping started the "reform and opening up" policy, the size of the US economy was approximately 31.5 times that of China. In 2002, the size of the US economy (US$9.22 trillion) was only 7.6 times larger than China's (US$1.21 trillion). The gap is expected to shrink further if China sustains its current growth rate (Wang,Yuan-Kang 2006).

By 2020, India will have a population of 1.3 billion and the third largest GDP in the world in purchasing power parity terms (US$13.3 trillion) as against its current fourth position. It will emerge as the second most important economic powerhouse in Asia by 2020, next only to China. India's rise will be driven by knowledge-based industries and services (Hussain, Javid).

India and China will also be the major driving forces for stimulating world economic growth over the next 25 years and beyond. The United States, China and India will together account for more than 50 per cent of global economic growth between 2005 and 2020, with Asia's overall share of the world economy rising to 43 per cent from its current 35 per cent (www.atimes.com).

Other aspects of the India–China success story are:

1. Overall, both China's and India's GDP will grow at an annualized rate of 6 per cent.
2. By 2020, China's economy, measured at PPP exchange rates will be on par with the United States.
3. China's share of global consumer spending will nearly triple in the next 15 years.
4. Asia will be the largest consumer region in overall terms. For example, by 2020, Asia is projected to account for 38 per cent of all auto sales, nearly double the current level.
5. Some 471 million net new workers will enter the global workforce, with China alone accounting for 65 million of these. India will account for a remarkable 142 million, with the United States as the third-largest contributor with 12.5 million workers. The European Union will experience growth of 8.4 million workers (The overwhelming majority of new US and EU jobs will be in the service industry.)
6. Asia will move on from being just the manufacturing center of the world. Its knowledge workers performing complex roles requiring developed communication and judgment skills are expected to be in great demand.

4.2 Strategic Implications

The report of the US National Intelligence Council [NIC] entitled: *Mapping the Global Future*, predicted the emergence of China and India as new major global players by 2020, which "would transform the geopolitical landscape" and have implications similar to those of the rise of unified Germany in the 19th century and of the United States in the

20th century (National Intelligence Council, 2004). The report suggested that the United States' relative power position would be eroded not only by the rise of China and India but also that of other countries such as Brazil and Indonesia.

The report focused particularly on the implications of these developments for Asia. It pointed out that China would offer Asian states an appealing vision of national security, an order in which the United States would have to compete with more attractive offers. Failing this, China would create its own regional security that would exclude the United States (Kaplan, Fred, 2005). China has already begun to boost its linkages with various partners. In recent remarks, Chinese President Hu Jintao has said, "In 2020, China's economy will integrate still more closely with the Asian economy, giving rise to a new type of partnership characterized by mutual benefits and mutual assistance[1]".

These partnerships help China in two ways: first, to find a middle ground between traditional allies and adversaries thereby enabling China to take care of her concerns without any kind of direct confrontation with the USA; second, it can accomplish her purpose by linking economic benefit with bilateral relations.

Such partnerships, commentators have noted, are open to potential allies and adversaries and recognize national differences in culture, ideology and interests while seeking to build mechanisms to manage areas of potential conflict (Wang, Yuan-Kang 2006).

The best examples of these partnerships are those that China has with Russia and ASEAN. With Russia, China has a close defence and energy relationship. Both are working in tandem to counter American penetration in Central Asia. Again China has engaged the Central Asian countries through the Shanghai Cooperation Organization (SCO). With ASEAN, China has greatly broadened and deepened its ties over the

[1] Quoted in Hu Xiao, "China to quadruple GDP by 2020 to $4 trillion," *China Daily*, October 24, 2006 (www.chinadaily.com.cn).

last 10 years, both in the economic and political areas including the promise of a China–ASEAN Free Trade Area by 2015, so much so that some observers believe it is viewed more favourably than the United States, and possibly even as a counterweight to the United States.

4.3 Sino–Indian Relations

As a means for China and India to achieve their projected status, observers have highlighted the importance of "political statesmanship and diplomatic foresight on the part of the two in managing domestic issues and international relations with the United States and other member countries of the Security Council as well as with their politically hostile neighbours.[2] They have also suggested that it would be ideal for regional and global prosperity and peace for China and India to set the stage for a strategic partnership to improve their bilateral political, economic, social and security relations and to act in concert at global and regional forums, to promote greater economic and political cooperation in Asia.

The emerging global and Asian political and economic scenario has placed India in an enviable position. The commentator C. Raja Mohan, (Raja Mohan, C. 2006) has described it thus:

> India is now emerging as the swing state in the global balance of power. In the coming years, it will have an opportunity to shape outcomes on the most critical issues of the twenty-first century: the construction of Asian stability, the political modernization of the greater Middle East, and the management of globalization.

Today, India is seen as a valuable partner by all the principal international players: be it United States, Russia,

---

[2] As quoted in Event Report on the Seminar "India-China 2020: Great Leap Forward," led by Dr. Charan Wadhva and Zhang Jun, *Foreign Policy Centre*, London, March 23, 2005, 7–8; (www.fpc.org.uk/fsblob/425.pdf).

China and the European Union. Given its sustained democratic and secular polity over 60 years, which in the contemporary scenario has acquired a new salience, India is automatically on the right side of the values of globalization, which espouses democracy, respect for human rights and multiculturalism, and rejects extremism and violence. Not surprisingly, India is a key player not only in various regional and continental groupings, but also in the East Asia Summit, the Shanghai Cooperation Organization and the expanding ASEAN.

Till recently, Sino–Indian ties had been constrained by the unresolved border issue and China's strategic partnership with Pakistan. The scenario today is quite different. India has achieved considerable economic success and is seen as a major player on the regional and world stage, with robust and expanding relations with all the principal players and regional groupings. It would appear that the stage is set for China to take a fresh look at its ties with India. As two prominent commentators on the region have noted, "China's long-standing hostility to India is being transformed by Beijing's and Delhi's mutual interest in improving their trading and wider bilateral relations". They have also observed that Pakistan's alliance with the United States in the Global war on Terrorism (GWOT) and the Sino–Indian thaw have put unprecedented strain on the so-called 'time-tested friendship' between Pakistan and China" (Shaikh, Farzana and Owen Bennett Jones, 2006)

Objectively speaking, there is a strong rationale for robust Sino-Indian relations:

1. Both countries have a deep and abiding interest in maintaining the security and stability of Asia's principal hydrocarbon regions—West Asia and Central Asia. The dependence of the two countries for oil and gas supply from these two regions is expected to increase substantially despite attempts to diversify their sources.

2. Both countries share a common interest in combating Islamic extremism and violence and protecting their domestic populations from related terror threats carried out under the guise of jihad. Hence, both countries share concerns about the strong base provided to extremist elements in Pakistan.

3. Both countries are alarmed by the prevailing situation of a unipolar world. They share a deep concern about the instability and insecurity in West Asia stemming from the unilateral and militarist policies of the United States, and would support policies promoting multipolarity in world affairs.

4. Both countries have a profound interest in encouraging groupings within Asia to promote broad Asian economic cooperation and possibly even a strategic consensus. Such cooperation would be based on consultations within the Shanghai Cooperation Organization and the East Asia Summit, and could extend in due course to ASEAN. The low key trilateral dialogue between India, Russia and China could increase in importance over time.

5. Both countries have built up strong bilateral economic ties with a two-way trade already valued at US$20 billion in 2006 as against US$117 million in 1987. It is expected to increase to US$30 billion by 2009, though this could happen even earlier.

Energy has been a major factor in building up bilateral ties between India and China. Prior to the visit of Indian petroleum minister Mani Shankar Aiyar to China in January 2006, there had been a number of well-publicized occasions when Indian companies had been outbid by Chinese companies in the competition to acquire oil equity assets in different countries, including Angola, Kazakhstan and Nigeria. These events were given considerable prominence in the Indian and international media, highlighting the political aspects of the energy-related rivalry and feeding the international discourse that saw the pursuit of energy security in terms of competition and conflict.

Aiyar's visit was aimed at exploring with Beijing the possibilities of Indian and Chinese companies actually cooperating with each other in acquiring hydrocarbon assets abroad. He candidly told the Chinese that they had paid US$2 billion extra for their acquisition of assets only because Chinese and Indian companies had competed against each other. In his public remarks in Beijing, Aiyar stated:[3]

> Aggressive bidding by either party [India & China] only pushes up the price of the asset to the advantage of the seller and the disadvantage of both bidders. In the end, whether the winner is China or India, the buyer ends up paying more – and sometimes substantially more – than might have been the case if bidding against each other had been replaced, or at least moderated, by prior consultation.

Aiyar then went on to lay the foundation of an energy-based bilateral relationship in the following terms:

> It is in search of such mutual cooperation to the mutual benefit of our two countries that I have come to Beijing. My visit has been carefully prepared. The outcome has, therefore, been gratifying. For I have encountered here a ready willingness at the Ministerial and the company level *to engage China and India in a strategic and cooperative quest for energy security. For our part, we look upon China not as a strategic competitor but as a strategic partner.*
>
> Our cooperation in energy is based on equal cooperation, mutual benefit, mutual respect and enhanced understanding. [Emphasis added.]

He concluded his speech with these words:

> China has an excellent record of regional cooperation in Asia. So does India. Together, we can set the agenda for Asian energy cooperation. That is how *the Asian Quest for Energy Security could lead to Asia regaining its traditional place – a place it has held for thousands of years of recorded history*

[3] *See* www.countercurrents.org/ind-aiyar170206.htm.

and lost only in the last two hundred years or so – in the vanguard of the advancement of human civilization.

The Asian Renaissance brought us all to independence and liberation. Now, the Asian Resurgence depends on energy cooperation in Asia. The 21st century will indeed be the Asian century only if Asian countries — buyers or sellers — join hands together in a continent-wide bid at bringing Asia together and keeping Asia together. I am confident that we will. [Emphasis added.]

Conclusion

Among the world's energy commentators, there is unanimity about just one aspect of energy security—that it is central to contemporary global economics and politics. On every other aspect there is debate and contention, with votaries on all sides being vociferous in their assertions and usually uncompromising in their positions. These debates range across all aspects of the energy value chain and include issues of: interdependence *versus* competition; geopolitics *versus* sustainability; fossil fuels *versus* renewables, oil boon *versus* oil curse; pros and cons of nuclear power; West Asia as a reliable supplier *versus* the need to diversify sources; and human development needs *versus* ecological interests.

Such debates are natural since issues of energy security, although under discussion for several decades (particularly, after the oil shocks of the 1970s) have only acquired a broader global salience in recent years. Earlier, energy issues had primarily concerned the developed countries (usually IEA members), who were in contention with the OPEC member countries and whose interactions generally led to a mutually acceptable equilibrium in the global oil economy. With the emergence of Asian consumers, particularly the developing countries of China and India, and the promise of considerable hydrocarbon potential in Central Asia, Saharan and Sub-Saharan Africa, the global energy economy has been fundamentally transformed, so that exclusivist IEA–OPEC arrangements are no larger sustainable, and the needs of new players need to be accommodated. This has created a certain disorder in the global hydrocarbon situation, even as IEA members, led by the United States, are desperately attempting to cope with the perceived "threat" to the arrangements with OPEC and non-OPEC producers that had hitherto sustained their political interests, their growth rates and their lifestyles.

What has further complicated the global energy scenario and given it a sharper competitive edge is the fact that these significant changes are taking place in a post-9/11 environment marked by insecurity, instability and uncertainty. The neoconservatives had used this national catastrophe to implement their agenda of US domination over world affairs, particularly in West and Central Asia, through the robust pursuit of policies of intervention, intrusion and hegemonic domination based on the unilateral use of force.

These policies are being pursued under the label of the global war on terror (now re-christened the "long war") to bring reform, human rights and democracy to these regions. Most observers, however, tend to view these interventions not as an agenda for positive and healthy transformation but a cynical plan to suit US strategic interests, which are largely centred on meeting its own energy needs and controlling the global energy economy. Hence, the pursuit of energy security through a global partnership is now given less attention as compared to the aggressive pursuit of self-centred geopolitical interests.

India recognizes that its own energy interests, on which its national economic development rests, require it to pursue policies of accommodation and cooperation with the principal producers and consumers of Asia. Accordingly, it has an immediate interest in the security and stability of West Asia and Central Asia. To realize these interests, it needs to pursue long-term strategic energy partnerships with the major producers, and to cooperate with the principal Asian consumers—China, Japan and Republic of Korea. India is aware that this cooperation with Asian producers could be obstructed and even jeopardized not just by historic fault lines between the principal Asian players but also by external players who could take advantage of these to deepen existing divisions and encourage contentions.

Asia has to overcome serious obstacles in promoting cooperation projects. Through the second half of the last century, even as Europe pursued an agenda of intra-continental cooperation after the bloodletting of the previous 50 years, Asian regions and subregions were divided by Cold War arguments and affiliations, and in some cases became theatres where the big powers fought their proxy wars.

The last decade of the 20th century saw the emergence of the Central Asian republics as sovereign states, although West Asia and South Asia remained areas of fierce contention with violence perpetrated by state and non-state actors from within as also major external powers that intervened in pursuit of their interests. Thus, after over 250 years of colonial domination and internecine conflict, it is only in the last few years that Asian countries have begun to see the prospect of peace and the opportunity to pursue intra-continental interests in a relatively autonomous strategic space. It is not that long-standing bilateral issues involving the principal Asian states have been resolved. Indeed, in some cases, they have even been given a new resonance and continue to provide opportunities for outside players to intervene as hegemonic powers rather than benign partners.

However, the Asian scenario is not entirely bleak. Opportunities have also emerged to pursue its energy interests through cooperative ventures that include investments in upstream and downstream hydrocarbon projects, sustainability proposals and infrastructure projects, particularly transnational pipelines. Pipelines are particularly daunting in an Asian environment which has been the arena of considerable intra-continental discord and conflict, and has relatively few success stories in regard to regional and continental cooperation. It is also true that some issues that divide Asian countries, particularly neighbours, are fairly complex and are unlikely to be resolved in the near future.

While there are serious challenges in implementing transnational pipeline projects, the common interest of energy producers in having stable markets and for consumers to have assured supplies for their economic development programs imparts enduring attention and urgency to these projects. Though Asia has relatively little experience in transnational oil and gas pipelines, the availability of abundant hydrocarbons within the continent, coupled with the overwhelming demand for this resource, ensures that both national and energy security concerns can and should coalesce.

Moreover, such cooperative ventures are facilitated by the fact that, unlike the colonial era and the Cold War period, Asia currently has the technological, financial and human resources required to pursue these projects. Hence, not surprisingly, every multilateral grouping in Asia accords the highest importance to energy-related issues, in the confident hope that energy cooperation and interdependence could nurture peace and prosperity in Asia just as the European Coal and Steel Community laid the foundations for the European Union fifty-five years ago.

Will Asia be able to seize the present opportunity and utilize energy as the binding force to promote a positive agenda for the common benefit of its constituent countries? It is too early to give a categorically affirmative answer since only a few faltering steps have been taken towards cooperation and partnership. Turning to history for guidance, it might be recalled that sixty years ago, just before the nightmare of the Cold War, the peoples of Asia shared a brief shining moment when they envisioned an Asian renaissance after the demise of colonialism, at the Asian Relations Conference in New Delhi. In April 1947, four months before India gained independence and a few years before most other Asian countries became free, Jawaharlal Nehru set out this vision of an Asian rebirth:

> We stand at the end of an era and on the threshold of a new period of history...Asia after a long period of quiescence has suddenly become important in world affairs...Asia is again finding itself...The people of India welcome their fellow Asians from other countries to confer with them about the present and future, and lay the foundation of our mutual progress, well-being and friendship.

According to the Chinese delegate, "After years of foreign domination, under some form or other, liberty has dawned and the world is destined to see another renaissance in Asia." This vision of Asian renaissance may continue to offer a source of inspiration for current efforts.

Bibliographical References

Shelley, Toby (2005), *Oil Politics, Poverty and the Planet* (London: Zed Books Ltd., 2005) 103.

Noreng, Øystein (2006), *Crude Power-Politics and the Oil Market* (London: I.B. Tauris Publishers, 2006) xi.

Chellaney, Brahma (2007), "New Great Game," *The Asian Age*, New Delhi, June 2, 2007, 7.

Duck-Koo, Chung(2006), 'Asia Century—Northeast Asia, ASEAN and India: Complementarity and Survival Strategies,' *Eminent Persons Lecture,* RIS, New Delhi, 27 January 2006 (www.ris.org.in).

Hussain, Javid, Pakistan's likely shape in 2020,' *CSS Forums* (www.css.forum.com.pk).

Dr. Yuan-Kang Wang (2006), 'China's Great Strategy and US Primacy: Is China Balancing American Power?' *The Brookings Institution*, Washington, D.C, July 2006, 17; (www.brookings.edu)

(www.atimes.com), 'China, India moving ahead of the pack,' *Asia Times*, June 24, 2006.

National Intelligence Council, *'Mapping the Global Future: Report of the National Intelligence Council 2020 Project,'* Washington, DC, December 2004, 47.

Kaplan, Fred (2005), 'A CIA Report Predicts that American Global Dominance Could End in 15 Years,' *Global Policy Forum*, January 26, 2005 (www.globalpolicy.org).

Raja Mohan, C. (2006), 'India and the Balance of Power,' *Foreign Affairs*, vol. 85, no. 4, July–August 2006, 17.

Shaikh, Farzana and Owen Bennett Jones, (2006), 'Pakistani foreign policy under Musharraf: Between a rock and a hard place,' *Briefing Paper* ASP BP 06/01 (London: Chatham House, March 2006, 2 (www.chathamhoue.org.uk/viewdocument.php?documentid=7349).

5

China's Recent Efforts in International Energy Cooperation

ZHOU XINGBAO

Despite the rise in world oil prices, China is a big energy consumer and it relies mainly on its domestic supply of energy. With the sharp hike in the oil prices in the international market recently, some people have been blaming China's increased oil consumption and import for the rise of oil price. With its fast growing economy, China has become a big energy consumer in the world. As the most populous country in the world and with such a big economy, China has to be and is also entitled to consume more energy. Yet at present, China's per capita energy consumption is only 84 per cent of the world average, its per capita oil consumption is only half of the world average and its per capita oil import only 37 per cent of the world average. The US per capita oil consumption is 14 times that of China. To meet the needs of its huge population and growing economy is it reasonable that China should use more energy?

China is also a big energy producer, apart from a large producer of coal. Coal is the main energy source used in China occupying nearly 70 per cent of China's total energy consumption and this will remain so in future too. China became a net oil importer in 1993 and its oil import has increased since then. China continues to be a significant oil producer in the world and the import of oil is still kept under 50 per cent of its total oil consumption. On the whole, China is still supplying and will continue to supply over 90 per cent of its energy consumption from out of its domestic resources. Therefore, China is not and cannot be the reason for the oil price rise in the world.

China is a responsible and active participant in the international energy cooperation and is playing an important constructive role in the international energy cooperation. To illustrate this, I will list very briefly here the actions taken by the Chinese Government in the past months alone:

> On June 7, Vice Minister Zhang Guobao for China's National Development and Reform Commission participated in the Second Five-State Energy Ministers' Meeting in Japan. The Meeting issued a joint statement in which the five major Asia-Pacific oil-consuming countries expressed great concern for the soaring crude oil prices. Vice Minister Zhang appealed to the countries participating in the meeting to face the problems existing in the international oil market, strengthen their cooperation in coping up with the excessive speculation in the market and try to keep the oil market stable and predictable. Actually, this mechanism of the Energy Ministers' Meeting among the five countries, namely, China, US, India, Republic of Korea and Japan, was initiated by China and its first meeting was held in Beijing in December, 2006.

On June 18, the Fourth China-US Strategic and Economic Dialogue was held in the US. The two sides signed a 10-year Energy and Environment Cooperation Framework. This marked an important step forward in the cooperation between the two countries in the development of energy and protection of environment and it will also exert a positive impact on the global energy cooperation.

On June 19, the Governments of China and Japan reached an understanding on the East China Sea Issue. The two sides agreed and selected a block in East China Sea for common exploitation without undermining the legal positions of each other. This significant first step shows that China and Japan have the capability and sincerity to properly handle the sensitive issue of the East China Sea. The settlement of the issue will be beneficial for the cooperation between the two countries in the field of energy development and will also be in the interest of the entire world.

On June 20, the Chinese Government raised the retail prices of diesel oil and gasoline in China by almost 18 per cent. It was a significant act to curtail the consumption of oil and to stimulate the energy production and conservation in China.

On June 22, China's Vice-President Xi Jinping during his first visit abroad after taking over the office of Vice-President attended the International Energy Conference held in Jeddah, Saudi Arabia. In his speech, he expounded China's energy strategy in depth and called upon all the oil producing and consuming countries to strengthen their dialogue and cooperation and adopt comprehensive measures in order to strike a balance between world energy demand and supply and maintain world energy security. These acts regulated by the Chinese Government in such a short time show that China is making great efforts to promote international energy cooperation for the benefit of the entire world.

5.1 Six Principles of China's Energy Strategy

In recent years China has put forward and emphasized the concept of scientific development and the concept of harmonious and coordinated development. From what China has done in recent years and activities of the Chinese Government in just one short month recently as listed above, it can be clearly seen that in the energy field, China is sticking to and will continue to stick to the following six principles:

1. Both energy exploitation and energy conservation are to be emphasized but priority is given to energy saving. In 2006, at the National People's Congress a goal was set up to reduce China's energy consumption per unit of GDP by 20 per cent from the 2005 level by 2010. Although this is a difficult task to fulfill, marked progress has been made in this regard. In 2004, China's GDP increased by 10.1 per cent, while its energy consumption increased by 16.1 per cent. In 2006, for the first time, rate of energy consumption increase in China was lower than its rate of GDP growth. And, in 2007, while its GDP increased by 11.4 per cent its energy consumption increased only by 7.8 per cent and its oil consumption only increased by 6.3 per cent.

2. China will continue to rely mainly on its domestic energy supply. Its domestic energy supply still has very great potential. Its coal reserves are abundant, its hydroelectric sources are huge, and its renewable energy sources such as wind, solar etc. are only beginning to be tapped. China will be able to meet the demands for economic growth and the improvement of people's life mainly by increasing its domestic energy supply.

3. Diversified development of energy sources will be pursued. China will try to optimize its energy mix and make great efforts to develop all the available forms of energy such as coal, oil and gas, hydroelectricity, nuclear power, wind electricity, solar energy, etc. These various forms of energy will supplement each other and secure a stable energy supply.
4. Reliance on science and technology will be emphasized. China will encourage all the technological progress and innovation in the energy field to raise its efficiency in energy use and to seek new ways to exploit energy resources. China's efficiency in energy use is still very low compared with the advanced developed nations, so it has great potentials to improve itself in this field.
5. China will protect the environment in its energy development. China has set the aim of building a resource-conserving and environment-friendly society. Therefore it will coordinate its energy production with environment protection meticulously so as to ensure the country's sustainable and scientific development. For example, China has shut down tens of hundreds of small thermal power plants that use coal as their fuel and caused serious pollution, although China on the whole still needs more electricity supply.
6. China will promote and strengthen mutually beneficial international energy cooperation. China will do its utmost to promote the win-win cooperation among the energy producing and consuming nations on the basis of equality and mutual benefit so as to ensure the balance between the energy supply and demand in the world and the energy security. Many of the acts of the Chinese Government I listed above are in line with this principle.

Energy is important for the development of entire mankind. The rational exploitation and sustainable development of energy are most significant for the growth of world economy and progress of the human society. The energy issue is a global concern. To strike a balance between world energy demand and supply and to maintain world energy security is an urgent common task for all the nations. China will firmly adhere to these six principles as listed above.

6

Energy Saving in the Japanese Industrial Sector and International Cooperation

YUJI MORITA

6.1 Abstract

The improvement of energy efficiency contributes to both the aspects of assuring stable supply of energy and preventing global warming. In addition, it may be expected that the measures can provide the effects of stimulating economy by calling the development of equipment allowing energy saving, by enhancing related investments, and by bringing in the opportunity to create new industries.

In Japan, energy saving has been promoted in the industrial sector as the results of two oil crises and the development of energy saving technologies has been activated. In particular, manufacturing industries have actively pursued energy saving activities for reducing costs to maintain the international competitiveness of products and for assuring the energy supply to maintain business activity.

For example, the share of the iron and steel industry as a representative energy intensive industry in Japanese final energy consumption was about 21 per cent in fiscal year 1973 when the first oil crisis occurred, but decreased to about 11 per cent in fiscal 2006. At the same time, the consumption of heavy fuel oil in the iron and steel industry decreased from 13.46 million kiloliters in fiscal year 1973 to 1.27 million kiloliters in fiscal year 2006.

The examples of representative energy saving technologies introduced into the energy intensive industries include CDQ (Coke Dry Quenching) in the iron and steel industry and the kilns equipped with NSP (New Suspension Preheater) in the cement industry. Since these technologies can significantly improve energy efficiency, if they are disseminated in the countries where such technologies have not been introduced yet, it may be expected that they will significantly contribute to the reduction in energy consumption and the reduction in CO_2 emission.

For these reasons, Japan promotes further reduction in energy consumption in global scale by disseminating these energy saving technologies in addition to bio-energy and photovoltaic power generation technologies through the activities of NEDO (The New Energy and Industrial Technology Development Organization) as a governmental organization and the APP (Asia-Pacific Partnership on Clean Development and Climate) as a multinational initiative.

6.2 Promotion of Energy Saving in the Japanese Industrial Sector

Energy saving contributes to both aspects of assuring stable supply of energy and preventing global warming. In addition, the measures can provide effects of stimulating economy by calling for the development of equipment allowing energy saving, by enhancing related investments, and by bringing in the opportunity to create new industries. Therefore, it may be expected that such measures can contribute to the realization of consistency between environment and economy.

In Japan, energy savings has been promoted in the industrial sector as a result of two oil crises and the development of energy saving technologies has been activated. When the second oil crisis occurred, Japanese exchange rate was about 250 yen/dollar and the share of petroleum import in total import trade reached up to 43 per cent due to the jump in crude oil price. The efforts to reduce energy cost became the center of interest in manufacturing industries and the trend triggered actions to improve energy efficiency. (Figure 6.1).

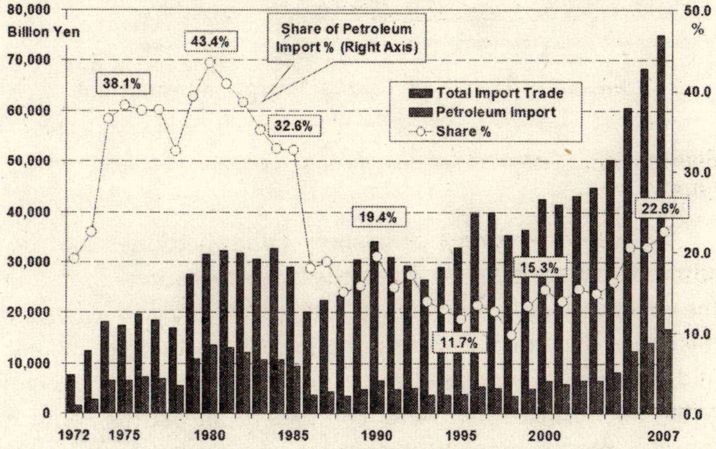

Fig 6.1 : Trends of Petroleum Import

Source: Data compiled from Petroleum Association of Japan

The increase in energy cost causes build up pressure of product cost and thereby degrades mutual and international competitiveness. The motivations to maintain international competitiveness of products and the assurance of energy supply to maintain production enhanced efforts to improve energy efficiency and to move towards value added products. At the same time, due to concerns for stable supply of oil, actions such as the reduction in dependency on oil by diversification to other energy resources including coal and natural gas were implemented (Figure 6.2).

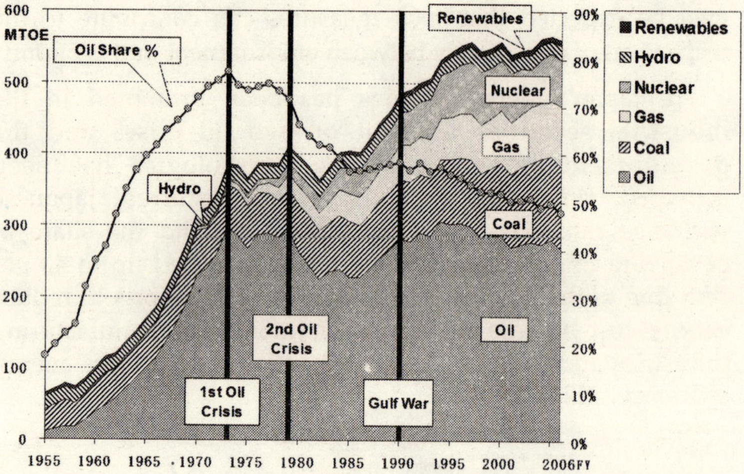

Fig 6.2 : Trends of Japan's Energy Consumption by Type of Energy

Source: *IEEJ, Handbook of Energy and Economic Statistics in Japan 2008*

To improve energy efficiency, initial activities had been commenced mainly by implementing measures that allow the enhancement of efficiency with relatively low cost. Such measures included covering piping with thermal insulator and control of temperature or processing time in reactors. After such measures were completed, measures requiring investment for more cost such as the renewal of facilities with higher efficiency were taken.

For example, the iron and steel industry is a representative energy intensive industry and its energy consumption occupies about 11 per cent of Japanese final energy consumption and about 26 per cent of the energy consumption in manufacturing industry sector in fiscal year 2006. However, in fiscal year 1973 when the first oil crisis occurred, the share was about 21 per cent of final energy consumption and about 36 per cent of the energy consumption n manufacturing industry sector (Figure 6.3).

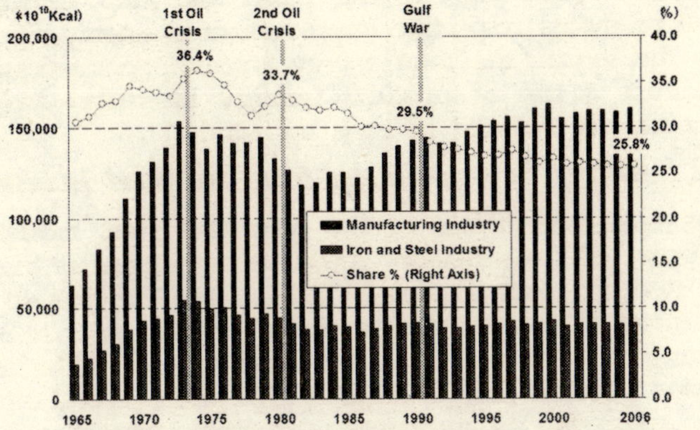

Fig 6.3 : Trends of Energy Consumption in Iron and Steel Industry

Source: *IEEJ, Handbook of Energy and Economic Statistics in Japan 2008*

But, the production of crude steel showed only a slight decrease from about 120 million ton in fiscal year 1973 to about 118 million ton in fiscal year 2006. Therefore, the decrease in the share of energy consumption by the iron and steel industry can be regarded as a result of the improvement of energy efficiency attained during the period. (Figure 6.4). Other industries regarded as energy intensive

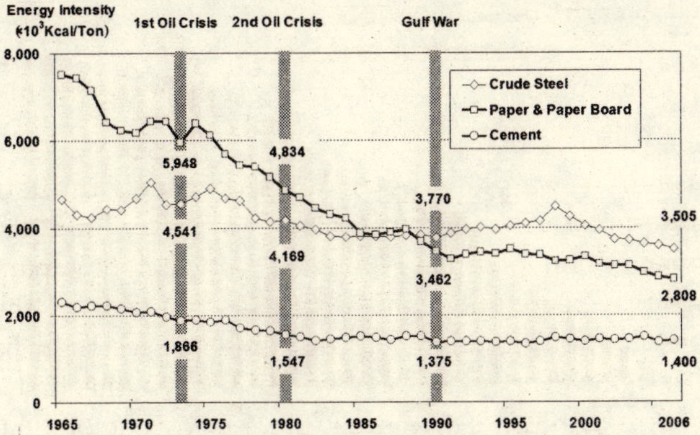

Fig 6.4 : Trends of Energy Intensity in Iron and Steel, Cement, Paper and Pulp Industries

Source: *IEEJ, Handbook of Energy and Economic Statistics in Japan 2008*

industries including ethylene, paper and pulp, cement, etc. also promoted respective improvement of energy efficiency. As the sequal, the total energy consumption necessary to produce a ton of product (energy intensity) has been significantly reduced in each industry.

6.2.1 Energy Savings in the Iron and Steel Industry

The full-scale efforts of the iron and steel industry to improve energy efficiency could be considered as triggered by two oil crises. Especially 1973, when the first oil crisis occurred, it is referred as so-called the first year of energy saving in Japanese iron and steel industry. During the period from the first oil crisis in 1973 to the second oil crisis, the energy saving measures were implemented mainly by operational improvement such as the reduction in the throughput of reductant agents for blast furnace and the reduction in fuel throughput for furnace.

During the period from the second oil crisis to the mid 1980s, large-scale investment for energy saving technologies was carried out. Thereby, TRT (Top Pressure Recovery Turbine) technology was developed, and large waste heat recovery facilities including the Sinter Cooler Waste Heat Recovery and CDQ (Coke Dry Quenching) plant in coke production process were introduced in a positive way (Figure 6.5).

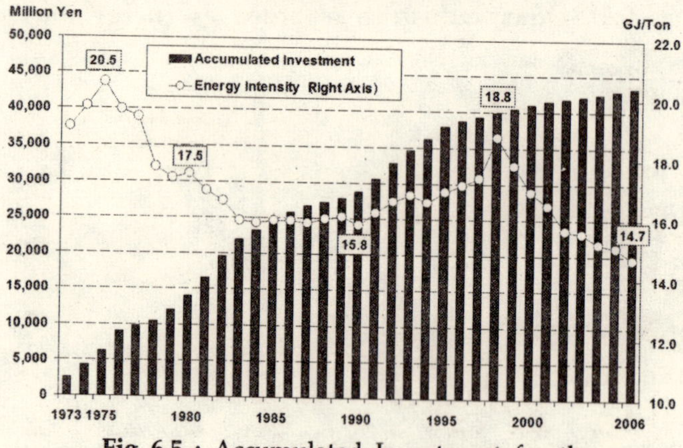

Fig 6.5 : Accumulated Investment for the Improvement of Energy Efficiency

Source: *Data compiled from the Japan Iron and Steel Federation*

In a coke furnace, coke is produced by loading coking coal into the furnace and heating (carbonizing) it to 900 – 1000°C under the oxygen free condition. Conventional technology (Coke Wet Quenching : CWQ) cools down the red-hot coke of 1000 – 1100°C pushed out from furnace by spraying water. The thermal energy of red-hot coke is lost as evaporation heat of water and coke dust is also dispersed.

In the CDQ process, red-hot coke pushed out from the coke furnace is carried to the top of coke cooling tower by bucket and loaded into it. Cooling gas (circulating inert gas) is blown into the bottom of the cooling tower and exchanges heat with red-hot coke. The coke cooled down to 200 – 250°C is discharged from the bottom of the cooling tower and carried by belt conveyor to blast furnace. On the other hand, inert gas heated up to 900–950°C is used for producing utility steam and electricity. The CDQ recovers 1.5 GJ of energy per ton of coke as steam (0.5 ton, 480°C, 60 atm). Since the CDQ uses cooling by gas circulated in a closed system, coke dust is not dispersed. Thus, the technology contributes to the reduction in usage of fossil fuel (Figure 6.6). At the same time, since the quality of coke is improved, the consumption of coke in blast furnace can be reduced by about two per cent.

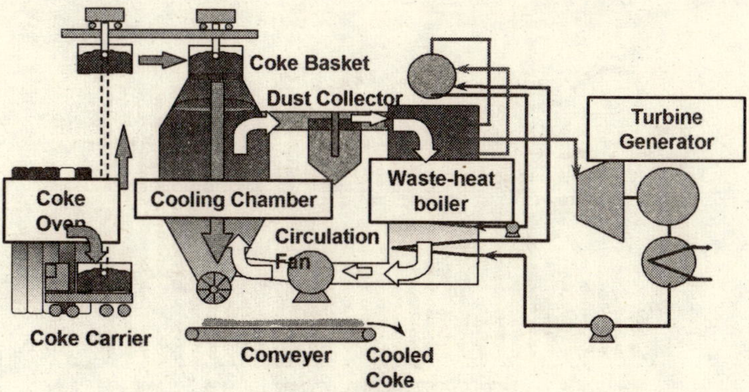

Fig 6.6 : CDQ Process

The iron and steel industry produces a lot of heat and by-product gas in the production process and products are produced by heating and cooling cycle. Hence, if any temperature drop in the process could be made as small as possible and if the production process could become continuous and simple, energy savings may be realized. Therefore, the industry has aggressively introduced large-scale technologies to recover and utilize the waste heat and energy and could enhance energy efficiency in whole process. Thereby, an energy savings of about 20 per cent could be realized at the beginning of the 1990s as compared in the early 1970s.

During the period from the mid 1980s to the mid 1990s, CC (Continuous Casting Plant), continuous annealing process, (PCI) pulverized coal injection technology, and coal moisture control (CMC) were introduced. The CC is a facility fabricating steel products such as slab, bloom and billet by using molten steel directly from a blast furnace. The PCI is a technology to enhance operational efficiency by directly injecting pulverized steam coal together with hot air through the inlet port of a blast furnace.

In the 1990s, higher added value of products was disseminated and more processes became necessary. As a result, since energy consumption increased, measures in the

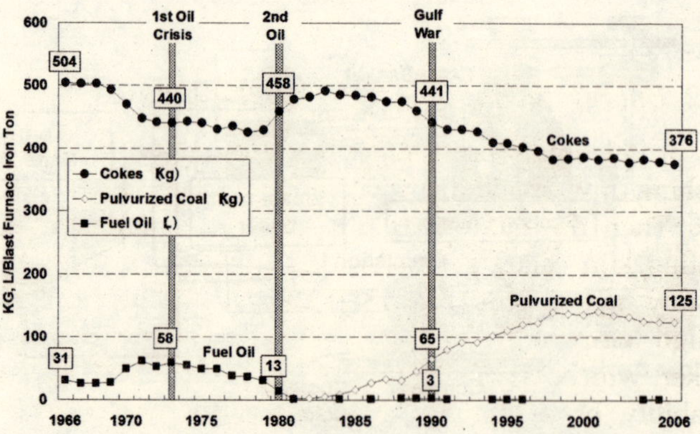

Fig 6.7 : Energy Consumption for Blast Furnace Iron Production

Source: *Data compiled from the Japan Iron and Steel Federation*

production process such as the enhancement of efficiency of private electric power generation facility were implemented and recycle of wastes such as waste plastics was actively promoted. In addition, the pulverized coal injection technology accelerated the conversion from oil to coal (Figure 6.7). The consumption of heavy fuel oil has been reduced from 13.46 million kiloliters in fiscal 1973 to 1.27 million kiloliters in fiscal 2006 (Figure 6.8).

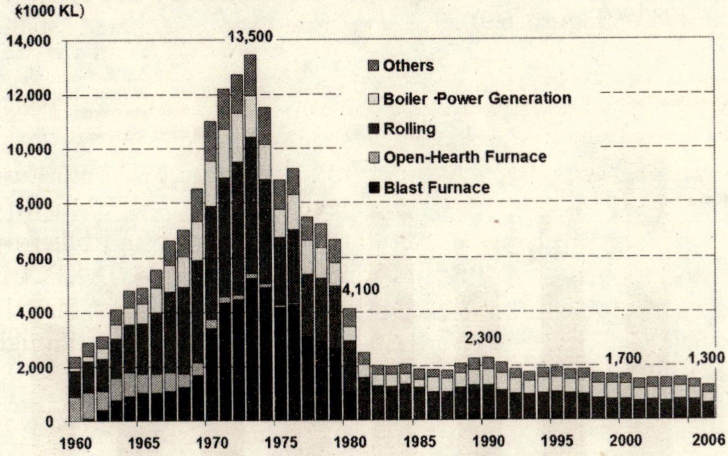

Fig 6.8 : Trends of Fuel Oil Consumption in Iron and Steel Industry

Source: *Data compiled from the Japan Iron and Steel Federation*

6.2.2 Energy Savings in the Cement Industry

The production process of cement begins with mixing and crushing raw materials such as limestone, clay and silica rock. Then the mixture is calcined and sintered in a large rotating kiln called a rotary kiln. In the calcination process, the raw materials are subjected to gradual chemical reaction at high temperature of about 1450°C or higher and becomes clinker which is the aggregate of compounds having the capability of hardening with water. In the finishing step after the calcination process, gypsum is added to adjust the hardening speed of cement and finally portland cement is produced by crushing these mixture to fine powder.

Wet type kiln had originally been utilized as the calcination and sintering process for cement production. For wet type kiln, the slurry like material for calcination and sintering was prepared by adding water to raw materials and then crushing it in a crusher. To improve thermal efficiency, dry method, in which energy consumption is only half of that for the wet type process, was invented and all the wet type kilns in Japan were replaced by dry type in the 1980s (Figure 6.9)

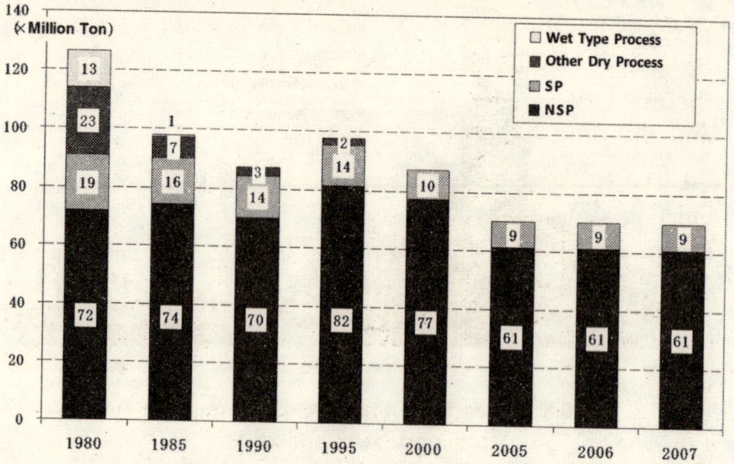

Fig 6.9 : Trends of Cement Production Capacity by Type of Kiln

Source: *Data compiled from Japan Cement Association*

Energy in cement production is mainly consumed as heating energy in the drying and calcination/sintering process of raw materials and as electric power in the crushing process of both raw materials and final products. Since about 70 per cent or more of the energy in whole production process are consumed in the heating process of calcination/sintering to obtain clinker, any energy saving measures and technical improvement in this process may realize significant effects in saving energy.

To further enhance the efficiency in the calcination/ sintering process of cement, rotary kilns equipped with SP (Suspension Preheater)/NSP (New Suspension Preheater)have been introduced. These facilities feed raw materials into a rotary kiln after passing through the preheating zone utilizing waste heat from the rotary kiln. The SP kiln installs a preheater consisting of cyclones of 4 – 5 stages. While waste gas from the kiln flows from lower stage to upper stage of the series of cyclones, pulverized raw material is loaded into the upper stage and subjected to the cycle of heat exchange and collection in each stage. The raw material is partly calcined in such process and then fed into the kiln. Because waste heat from the kiln is utilized efficiently, thermal efficiency is excellent. Also, the process is stabilized and the product quality is improved.

The NSP installs auxiliary calciner between SP and kiln. Since this method feeds raw materials into kiln after further calcination of raw materials than that of the SP kiln, its capability of calcination/sintering is improved to about twice that of the SP kiln. Also, hot waste gas of 350–380°C from the SP or NSP is utilized for drying raw materials or for electricity generation.

After the oil crises, conversion to these furnaces with higher efficiency has been promoted in Japan and thereby during 20 years from 1970 to 1990 the intensity for fuel usage and the intensity for electric power usage have been improved by 36 per cent and 18 per cent respectively. As the result, energy efficiency of highest level could be realized (Figure 6.10). At the same time, to lower the dependency on oil and to reduce energy cost, transfer from oil to coal has been carried out (Figure 6.11).

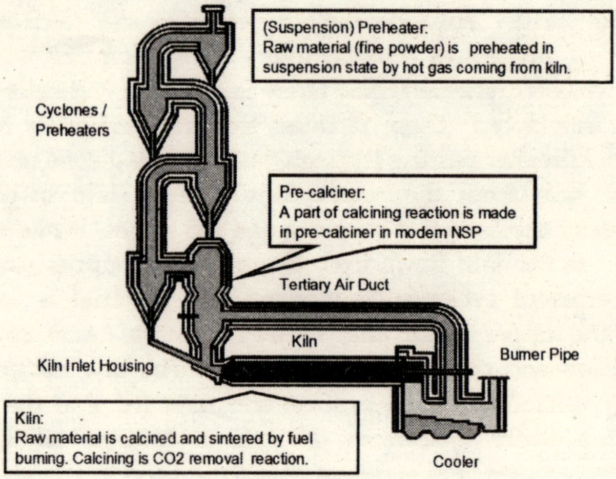

Fig 6.10 NSP Kiln

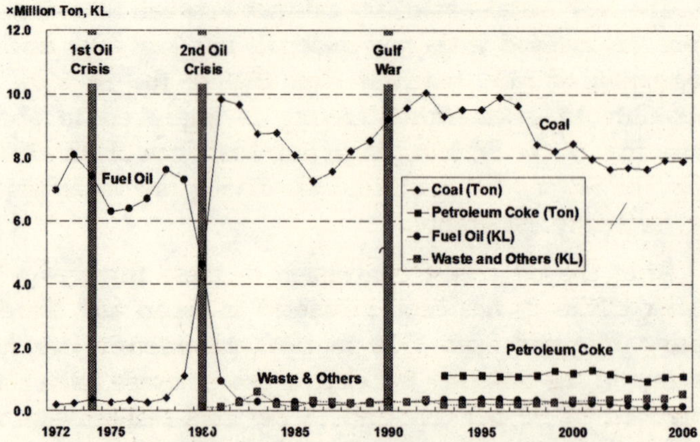

Fig 6.11 : Trends of Energy Consumption by Type of Energy

Source: *Data compiled from Japan Cement Association*

Because the conversion to these furnaces was 100 per cent completed by fiscal year 1997 in Japan, measures such as recovering waste heat or enhancing heat exchange efficiency have approached saturation level. Theoretically, energy consumption necessary to produce a ton of clinker is about 1.8 GJ. Today, energy efficiency of dry type kiln has been lowered to 2.9 – 3.0 GJ/t (Figure 6.12), near here and thus recent energy intensity remains almost constant (Figure 6.13).

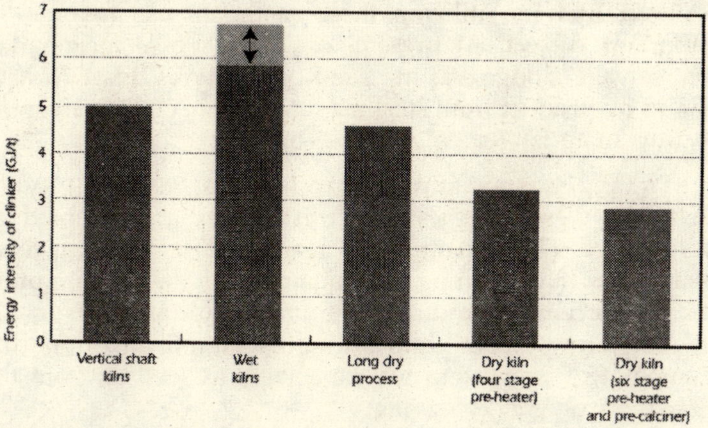

Note: For Wet Kilns, the arrow represents the range of energy consumption for different wet kiln types.

Source: *FLSmidth, 2006.*

Fig 6.12 : Energy Efficiency of Various Cement Clinker Production Technologies

Source : *IEA, Tracking Industrial Energy Efficiency and CO_2 Emissions, 2007*

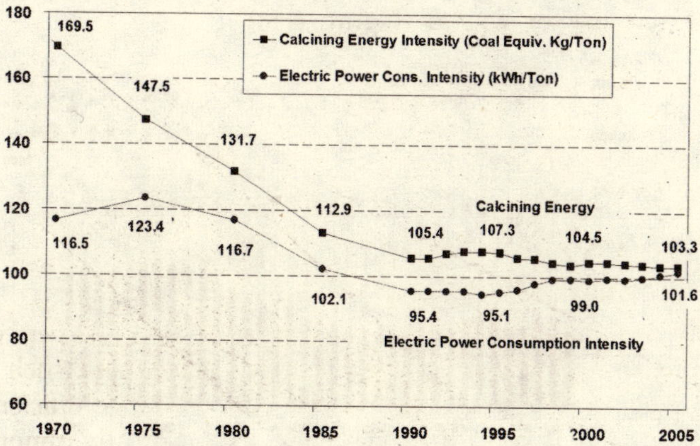

Fig 6.13 : Trends of Energy Intensity in Cement Production

Source: *Data compiled from Japan Cement Association*

However, wastes such as waste plastics, tyres, etc. and industrial by-products such as blast furnace slag, fly ash, etc. can also be used as fuel. Therefore, reduction in usage of fossil fuel by utilizing these materials has become an important subject. At present, coal ash, refuse incineration ash, sewage sludge, casting sand, waste tyres, blast furnace slag as by-product from steel manufacturing, etc. are accepted as raw material for calcination/sintering.

Today, wastes and by-products of over 20 types including waste plastics and waste tyres are accepted as heat source. Their quantity has reached 30,900 tons in fiscal year 2006. If converting this quantity to the consumption per ton of cement produced, the proportion amounts to 423 kg. Therefore, their contribution is significant from the viewpoint of promoting recycle society as well as from the viewpoint of energy saving.

However, the expansion of utilization of wastes, etc. may become a factor of degrading intensity for electric power due to the essential facilities for raw material/fuel pretreatment and the measures to transport them in the plant. While the proportion of the utilization of private electric power generation in the cement industry is greater than 60 per cent, the recent increase of the intensity for electric power may be considered as originating from increased use of wastes (Figure 6.14).

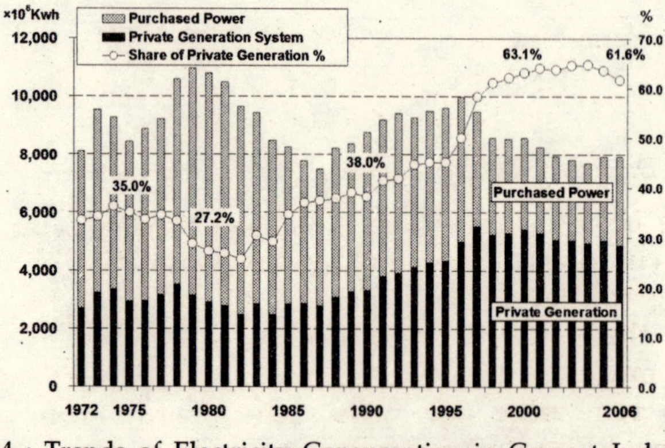

Fig 6.14 : Trends of Electricity Consumption in Cement Industry

Source: *Data compiled from Japan Cement Association*

6.2.3 Energy Savings in the Paper and Pulp Industry

Because the paper and pulp industry is considered as one of the energy intensive industries, the industry is actively promoting measures to save energy. While the industry uses renewable energy and energy from wastes, about 60 per cent of the total energy throughput is provided by fossil energy (Figure 6.15). Therefore, the paper and pulp industry has introduced black liquor as boiler fuel. Black liquor is a by-product when producing pulp from wood and mainly consists of components such as resin. Black liquor is also useful as carbon neutral energy.

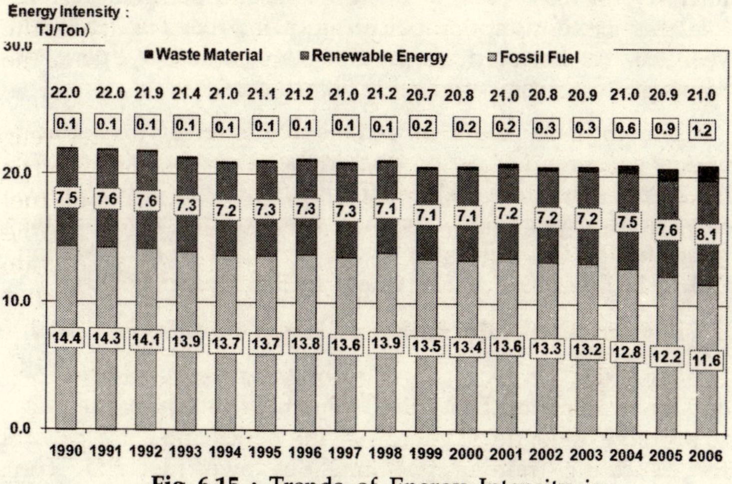

Fig 6.15 : Trends of Energy Intensity in Paper and Pulp Industry

Source: *Data compiled from Japan Paper Association*

The industry also operates biomass boilers using wood scrap, cut down trees, and waste materials for fuel by utilizing the feature as paper and pulp plant. To further reduce the usage of fossil energy together with energy saving measures, the industry promotes the conversion of fuel to renewable energy and the energy from wastes including RPF (Refuse Paper and Plastic Fuel) and waste tires. In recent years, the investment for diversification to such fuel is increasing.

From the viewpoint of energy savings, the recycle use of recovered paper is very important. Thus, its blending rate of recovered paper reached 60.6 per cent in fiscal 2006. On the other hand, higher utilization of recovered paper may cause difficulty because the quantity of black liquor obtained when producing flesh pulp decreases.

Since a paper and pulp plant uses low and medium pressure steam in the process, the co-generation system to generate electricity by using high pressure steam from boiler is widely introduced. In addition, through the measures including the introduction of energy saving type manufacturing facility and the alternative usage of mechanical pulp, the intensity for fossil energy consumption and the intensity for total energy consumption per product of paper pulp in fiscal year 2007 has been reduced by 20.6 per cent and 17.2 per cent respectively as compared with fiscal year 1990.

The industry aims to reduce the intensity for fossil energy consumption per product in the period of 2008 to 2010 by 20 per cent from 14,369 MJ/t in fiscal year 1990 (11,407 MJ/t in fiscal year 2007). The industry also aims to reduce the intensity for CO_2 emission by 16 per cent from 0.998 ton CO_2/t in fiscal 1990 (0.823 CO_2/t in fiscal year 2007).

6.3 Promotion of International Cooperation

In May 2006, "China - Japan Forum on Energy Conservation and Environmental Protection" was held in which the way to promote dialogue on energy saving policy and cooperation for educating/training personnel, etc. was decided. The direction of cooperation for energy savings in the private business sector including the establishment of joint ventures was set forth.

In addition, by the request from China, "The Five-Party Energy Ministers Meeting", at which the energy ministers from 5 countries, the US, China, Japan, India, and the Republic of Korea was held in December 2006. These five countries consume half of the global energy consumption. In the meeting, the joint statement incorporating the promotion of energy savings and the strengthening of emergency response, etc. was concluded.

In "The Second East Asia Summit (EAS)" held in January 2007, Japan expressed following cooperative initiative.

1. promote energy saving (accept 1,000 trainees in the next 5 years and establish "Asia Energy Efficiency and Conservation Collaboration Center," etc.)
2. promote biomass energy (accept 500 trainees in the next 5 years, etc.)
3. utilize coal in clean manner (construct "Coal Liquefaction Assistance Center" etc.)
4. dissolve the issue of energy poverty (implement the energy related ODA of 2 billion dollar in the next 3 years, etc.).

The summit adopted "Cebu Declaration on East Asian Energy Security" describing the establishment of the target for energy savings and the action plan, the promotion of biofuel usage, etc.

In August 2007, "The first EAS Energy Ministers' Meeting (EMM1) " was held in Singapore. The Ministers commended the work undertaken by the EAS ECTF (Energy Cooperation Task Force) to successfully identify three energy cooperation work streams viz, energy efficiency and conservation (EE&C), energy market integration, and biofuels for transport and other purposes – as a starting point to focus their efforts and to work towards the goal of affordable, secured and sustainable energy at all economic levels.

In recognition that improving energy efficiency and conservation is one of the most cost-effective ways of enhancing energy security and addressing climate change, the ministers supported the EAS ECTF's recommendations to promote EE&C, and agreed to undertake concrete actions to implement them. The ministers further noted the ongoing work on the "EAS Energy Outlook" by the Economic Research Institute for ASEAN and East Asia (ERIA). (ERIA was formally established in June 2008 in Jakarta, Indonesia.)

The ministers also welcomed the launch of the Asia Energy Efficiency and Conservation Collaboration Centre (AEEC) established in Japan in April 2007.

6.3.1 Potential of Energy Saving

In the recent situation that the price of resources including crude oil rises remarkably, the assurance of stable energy supply is an indispensable prerequisite for developing countries as well as for advanced nations to secure the long term stable growth of economy. Although assurance of stable energy is an urgent subject for the countries showing rapid economic growth including China and India, energy efficiency in these countries is generally low and it may be considered that there is ample room for improvement.

According to IEA, if the efficient technologies already commercialized are popularized in global scale and thereby energy saving is promoted, it may be estimated that world energy consumption can be reduced by 600 – 900 Mt per year. The amount corresponds to about 18 – 26 per cent of energy consumption in the industrial sector. Similarly, it may be estimated that CO_2 of 1900 – 3200 Mt can be reduced per year. The amount corresponds to 19 – 32 per cent of CO_2 emitted from the industrial sector (Table 6.1)

	Low ? High Estimates (Final energy, includes overlap)	**Low ? High Estimates of Technical Savings Potential** (Primary energy, excludes overlap)			**Total Energy & Feedstock Savings Potentials**
	EJ/yr	EJ/yr	Mtoe/yr	Mt CO_2/yr	%
Sectoral Improvements					
Chemicals/petrochemicals	4.0 ? 11.0	5.0 ? 6.5	120 ? 155	370 ? 470	13 ? 16
Iron and steel	2.0 ? 4.0	2.3 ? 4.5	55 ? 108	220 ? 360	9 ? 18
Cement	2.2 ? 2.7	2.5 ? 3.0	60 ? 72	480 ? 520	28 ? 33
Pulp and paper	1.0 ? 2.4	1.3 ? 1.5	31 ? 36	52 ? 105	15 ? 18
Aluminium	0.1 ? 0.6	0.3 ? 0.4	7 ? 10	20 ? 30	. 6 ? 8
Other non-metallic minerals and non-ferrous metals	0.4 ? 0.8	0.5 ? 1.0	12 ? 24	40 ? 70	13 ? 25
System/life cycle Improvements					
Motor systems	2.6	6 ? 8	143 ? 191	340 ? 750	
Combined heat and power	4.5	2 ? 3	48 ? 72	110 ? 170	
Steam systems	3.3	1.5 ? 2.5	36 ? 60	110 ? 180	
Process integration	2 ? 5	1 ? 2.5	24 ? 60	70 ? 180	
Increased recycling	3 ? 4.5	1.5 ? 2.5	36 ? 60	80 ? 210	
Energy recovery	3 ? 4.5	1.5 ? 2.3	36 ? 55	80 ? 190	
Total		**25 ? 37**	**600 ? 900**	**1,900 ? 3,200**	

Table 6.1 : Savings from Adoption of Best Practice Commercial Technologies in Manufacturing Industries (Primary Energy Equivalents)

6.3.2 Bilateral Cooperation

In April 2007, Japan and China announced the "Joint Statement by Japan and the People's Republic of China on the Further Enhancement of Cooperation for Environmental Protection" concerning energy cooperation enhancement. Both sides affirmed their sincere efforts at tackling the global environmental issues affecting the two countries and agreed that they would strengthen their cooperation focusing on energy issues such as energy conservation, coal and nuclear power, including model projects for the promotion of energy conservation and environmental businesses, as well as bolster cooperation in multilateral frameworks including the promotion of energy conservation in the Asian region.

Also in April 2007, Japan and India decided the establishment of the "Japan–India Energy Dialogue". This focuses on promoting comprehensive cooperation in the energy sector as endorsed in "The Joint Statement toward Japan-India Strategic and Global Partnership" issued in December 2006. Both sides recognized the importance of promoting energy conservation in order to improve energy efficiency. Based on this recognition, both sides would reinforce cooperation in such areas as energy intensive industrial sectors through exchange of experts and capacity building, and through the voluntary formulation of energy efficiency goals and action plans, and related efforts,.

Both sides also recognized the importance of new and renewable energy from the standpoints of energy security and the importance of development of environmentally sound technologies to address climate change issues. Accordingly, both sides would explore the possibility of joint research and development of technologies for the implementation of common projects to promote the introduction of renewable energy.

6.3.3 International Cooperation on Energy Saving by NEDO

Japan has contributed to international cooperation through various activities including the dispatch of experts to other countries. In particular, NEDO (The New Energy and Industrial Technology Development Organization) promotes the model business by which the effectiveness of Japanese new energy and energy saving technologies is demonstrated mainly in developing Asian countries.

The objectives of the model business by NEDO are to introduce Japanese technologies for the efficient use of energy including the energy saving technologies of the Japanese industrial sector into developing countries, etc. and to establish and popularize such technologies through demonstration tests. In the model business, facilities and equipments that can contribute to economic development of the country as well as to the reduction in greenhouse gas emissions are selected. Such business is implemented under consultation and cooperation with the country. In addition, when disseminating these technologies, NEDO supports activities including maintenance work conducted by the developing country itself for the facilities and equipments installed in the model business, and implements personnel dispatch business (Green Helmet Projects) for proliferating the technologies to other related facilities.

For example, in the case of the CDQ, the Shougang Group Corp in China introduced the CDQ technology in 1997 – 2000 as the model business and replaced conventional CWQ (Coke Wet Quenching) facilities. Thereby, the company succeeded in reducing energy usage of its iron works and demonstrated the energy savings effect as high as 24,700 t/y in crude oil equivalent. According to the result, the effectiveness of the CDQ technology has been demonstrated. In its "Tenth 5 year Plan" in March 2001, Chinese government decided that CDQ should be installed in 60 per cent or more of the coke furnaces having production capacity greater than or equal to a million ton/y. "The China Iron and Steel Development Policy" in 2005 specified that newly installed coke furnaces should have the capacity with dimension of greater than or equal to 6.0 m in height and should install the CDQ facility. In 2006, Chinese government has taken up the CDQ technology in its "Comments for Implementation of Major 10 Priority

Projects" in the "National 11th Five-Year Plan". As of February 2007, Japanese CDQ has been introduced in 33 coke production facilities in China (Figure 6.16).

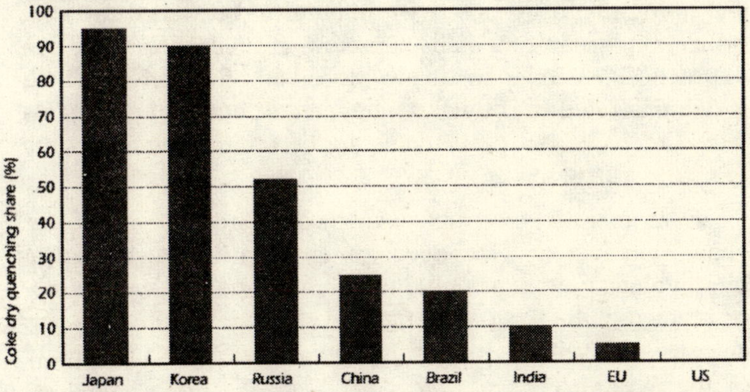

Sources: ISI Communication; Institute of Energy Economics Japan (IEEJ) (2006).

Fig 6.16 : Use of Coke Dry Quenching Technology

Source *IEA, Tracking Industrial Energy Efficiency and* CO_2 *Emissions 2007*

Following the popularization in China, NEDO sealed the basic agreements with the Indian government and Tata Steel in 2006 to introduce, demonstrate, and disseminate the CDQ technology also in the iron and steel industry of India and started the model business. The energy savings effect and the greenhouse gas reduction effect from the introduction of this technology are estimated as amounting to 50,000 t/y in crude oil equivalent and 137,000 t/y in CO_2 quantity, respectively.

Another technologies which NEDO is promoting in the model business include

1. Top Pressure Recovery Turbine (TRT) which uses the pressure of exhausted gas from the top of a blast furnace for power generation.
2. Cement Waste Heat Power Generation System which recovers the heat generated in cement calcination process for power generation

NEDO's another international project activities include the following:

Demonstration and dissemination of Japanese technologies for less environmentally burdensome coal utilization. Environmentally conscious clean coal technologies in practical use in Japan are introduced and their effectiveness is demonstrated in countries where environmental pollutants like SOx, NOx and particulates are becoming pervasive due to coal utilization.

Demonstrative research projects for photovoltaic power generation systems. The development and demonstration of photovoltaic power generation system technologies are jointly conducted with host countries, leveraging various climatic and social conditions to improve the durability and reliability of the systems.

Joint research projects with corporations, universities and research institutes of host countries. Cooperative research involves establishing and operating research facilities in counterpart countries, implementing joint research, and inviting foreign researchers to Japan. This program addresses specific issues in technology development and stimulates the indigenous research and development efforts of counterpart countries.

6.3.4 Activities of APP

APP (Asia-Pacific Partnership on Clean Development and Climate) is an initiative of regional cooperation started in 2005 and 7 countries, Japan, Australia, China, India, the Republic of Korea, the US and Canada, participate in the project. The objectives of the APP are to tackle issues including energy security and climate change by promoting regional cooperation for the development, dissemination, and transfer of clean and efficient technologies. These 7 countries occupy about half of the global economy, population, and energy consumption and 65 per cent of coal production, 48 per cent of steel production, 37 per cent of aluminium production, and 61 per cent of cement production.

Therefore, the cooperation of these 7 countries on energy savings is expected to significantly contribute to global energy savings. For the objectives, the following 8 task forces (TFs) promote activities by sector (Figure 6.17).

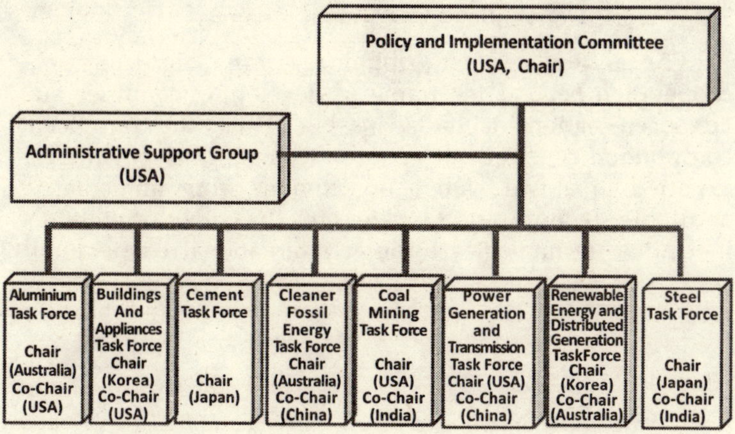

1. Aluminium
2. Buildings and Appliances
3. Cement
4. Cleaner Use of Fossil Energy
5. Coal Mining
6. Power Generation and Transmission
7. Renewable Energy and Distributed Generation

6.4. Action against Global Warming

In May 2007, Japan declared the objective that the country will reduce the emission of greenhouse gases by half until 2050 in "Beautiful Planet 50 (Cool Earth 50)" initiative. The government has shown the understanding that innovative technologies should be developed by efforts of international cooperation to tackle the problems at a global scale, and proposes the promotion of international cooperation including the sharing of technology road map through various existing international frameworks, the cooperation for technology development, and information sharing.

In July 2008, the 34th G8 Summit (Group of Eight Summit) was held in Hokkaido, Japan. With respect to the goal of achieving at least 50 per cent reduction of global emissions by 2050, the G8 leaders agreed to seek to share and adopt it with all Parties to the United Nations Framework Convention on Climate Change.

For action against global warming, international cooperation beyond the frame of developing countries and advanced nations is indispensable. Thus, the significant contribution of excellent Japanese technological potential is expected in a wide range of activities from immediately available technology transfer to the development of innovative technologies through international cooperation.

7

Malacca Straits and China's Energy Security

ZHAO HONGTU

Due to the rapid increase in energy demand and growing dependence on imported Middle Eastern and African oil, China has become increasingly vulnerable to disruptions of its oil supplies. In addition to the regional conflicts and the producers' embargo, any disturbance in Sea Lanes of Communication (SLOC) (especially the Malacca Straits), could also result in disruption of oil supplies. Unfortunately, the hotly debated "Malacca Dilemma" (or "Malacca Predicament") among some Chinese analysts has caused great concern for the outside world and has led to misperceptions about China's related policy and strategy.

The so-called "Malacca Dilemma" appears to be overstated. According to some analysts, the deep reliance on the Malacca Straits and the possible oil embargo by the United States makes China's maritime energy lifeline extremely vulnerable. Solution is, therefore, dependent upon the development of alternative mainland pipelines and expansion of the naval force to safeguard the energy shipments in an emergency. It is true that the Malacca Dilemma and other maritime energy transportation risks have already posed challenges to China's energy transportation, but it is not as serious as some people consider it to be. The main challenges to energy transportation are piracy, terrorism and transportation accidents in peace times rather than energy embargoes or sanctions in times of war.

While Daniel Yergin emphasized that Americans have a bias against China's energy demand, there is also a similar bias against the United States among the Chinese. For example, some analysts in China believe that the US intentionally does not allow China to access oil resources, and could disrupt China's oil supply routes on purpose, and that it influences transnational companies in disregarding China. In recent years, some reports on China's security of energy supply appearing in Chinese media have agreed that the major threats to China's energy security come from the United States, especially on issues like the marine transport route along the Malacca Straits. To some Chinese, America's embargo is more worrisome than piracy and transportation accidents.

During peace times, every merchant fleet has the right to sail through the choke points like the Straits of Malacca or Hormuz freely. The blockade against merchant fleets or oil tankers only takes place during war. "With more and more oil tanks shuttle those lines controlled by the American navy, some Chinese are more worried about American oil blockade"(Special Report: Chinese Companies abroad, 2005).

Due to globalization and ever-increasing economic interdependence between China and the US, it is unlikely that the US would impose oil blockades on China. China provides a big market for American exports. It is estimated that from 2000 to 2005, American exports to China increased by 160 per cent, at the same time it increased by only 10 per cent in other regions. It has been observed that half of the American companies' increased exports went to China (Council on Foreign Relations Report on US-China Relations). Moreover, America realizes that China's rapid economic growth is an important contributor to the growth of American and world economy. With the development of the global energy market, it is very difficult for the United States to achieve the goal of containing China's economic growth. Both China and United States need stable energy supplies at reasonable oil prices to sustain their economic growth. There is only one world of oil market. Any disruption of supply will affect the world market and harm the world economy, affecting even the United States adversely.

In terms of technology and practice, to pose an energy blockade, the United States also faces difficulties. It is almost impossible for US navy to cut off all of China's imports. According to Peter Van Doren of Cato Institute, it is very difficult to have an oil blockade, as it requires a large naval force along China's long maritime border, which is almost impossible (Juyan, Zhang, 2004). Other technical obstacles include: (a), to block or attack oil tankers in sea. It's very difficult to judge which of the oil tankers are owned by China or which of them have been hired from other countries; (b), blockage of choke points like Malacca Straits will also block the energy transportation of Japan and Korea; (c), about one quarter of the world merchant ships carry products that are made in China. Technically it's difficult to block China's oil tankers without affecting world trade. And also, once there is a blockage or sanction, it will be seen as an economy or trade blockage rather just an oil or energy blockage.

The energy embargo or blockade is mostly a show of political strength rather an economic one. In fact, even in the 1970s, when Arab countries imposed an oil embargo on the United States, the US still could get Arab oil through middlemen, albeit at a higher price. The real cause of limited gasoline supply in the United States was the Nixon Administration's oil price policy since August 1971 and not the OPEC's oil embargo (Peter Van, Doren, Jerry Taylor) only. Also, as a result of American sanctions against Libya and Iran, the oil companies from France, Italy and Spain took advantage of the vacuum and consolidated their position there. American sanctions against Cuba for several decades could not prevent Cuba from procuring necessary resources for itself, including oil.

In comparison to some major powers' oil embargo or blockade, a more realistic threat to energy transportation comes from piracy, terrorism, illegal arms trade and transportation accidents. Much of SLOC's concern has been about the effects of piracy and terrorism. Since the end of the Cold War, incidents of piracy increased from 6-7 annually before 1989 to 50 in 1991 and 469 in 2000. Southeast Asia is the region which has witnessed most piracy incidents. From 1991 to 2001, Southeast Asia had about 1600 piracy incidents that accounted for about 60 per cent of them across the world (Abhyankar, Jarant). After 9/11, attack on energy infrastructure has caused more concern. For example, a French oil supertanker rented by a Malaysian international petroleum company was attacked at Yemen's coast in 2002.

Intensified activity by the littoral states – Indonesia, Malaysia and Singapore – including coordinated patrols and 'eye in the sky 'aerial surveillance seems to have reduced the incidence of piracy, now increasingly limited to smaller vessels (Harris, Stuart 2007). According to ICC's Maritime Bureau report, the number of ships that were affected by piracy in 2006 decreased to 239 from 276 in 2005 and 329 in 2004. Around Indonesia, incidents of piracy dropped to 50 in 2006 from 79 in 2005 (Global Piracy Watch).

The terrorism remains a threat. The possibilities of sinking a large tanker to block the strait or blowing up an LNG tanker as well as a tactical nexus between pirates and terrorists cannot be ruled out but are generally thought unlikely, as is the possibility of blocking the straits given the width of the Malacca Straits even at their narrowest part (Harris, Stuart 2007).

Problems may arise from the added shipping capacity requirements. The transportation accidents in the Malacca Straits are about three times of the Suez Canal and five times of the Panama Canal. In 1975, there were oil tanker accidents leading to spillage of 80,900 tons of crude oil. In 1979, one oil tanker collided with a craft carrier leading to a leak of about 10,000 tons of crude oil. With the rapid growth of shipments but limited capacity of shipping, traffic accidents are likely to increase.

To minimise the risks associated with maritime energy transportation, the possibility of alternative routes – especially along the mainland pipeline routes – has been widely debated in China. Consequently, a number of proposals for building international mainland pipelines or bypassing routes became very popular. But the mainland pipeline has not reduced the risks that SLOC is facing. If some countries want to impose an oil embargo or a naval blockade, they also can do the same to mainland pipelines. And, in comparison to oil embargoes or blockades, cutting off the pipeline is much easier and cost-efficient. If piracy and terrorism are what people really worry about, pipelines also face a similar challenge, the only difference is that illegal armed forces indulge in piracy, since this happens quite often in Venezuela and Pakistan among other countries. At much higher economic cost, inflexibility and geopolitical competition will make the functioning of most of those proposed pipelines very difficult.

Even if some of the alternative pipelines came into existence, considering the rapidly growing import and economic costs, China's energy transportation will still very much rely on sea lines. However, in the event of an oil embargo or blockade, a decline in the number of incidents, or increasing cooperation for energy transportation routes, China needs to be more confident about its capability to deal with the remaining challenges and pay more attention to the creation of domestic infrastructure and improvement in the emergency response system, while pursuing regional cooperation.

As regards China's energy security policies and activities, the Malacca dilemma is one of the two most important issues (the other being Chinese national oil companies' overseas investment) that Western analysts are very much concerned about. What they most worry about is the naval buildup. According to some analysts, strengthening of the navy is necessary to safeguard security of the SLOC. It is true that some analysts talk about the Malacca dilemma in the visual as well as print media, but there are also a lot of different voices maintaining that the security of the sea lines or the Malacca dilemma is not a big deal and we should focus more on domestic issues and demand side management.

The grossly overstated "Malacca dilemma" is partly a result of the fact that the United States had imposed sanctions on China earlier, the possible large-scale American intervention when military conflict broke out in the Taiwan straits and also due to the contrast between the American and Chinese navies. Recently, the US tried to intervene militarily in the Malacca Straits to prevent China from cooperating with Middle East countries; it especially stalled a Chinese company's acquisition of an American oil company. These developments also added to China's worries. Some countries' increased involvement in the Malacca Straits also contributes a lot to the widespread "Malacca dilemma" among Chinese academics and media.

In addition to what has been explained above, "discussions ignoring market basics get more attention". Mixing wartime and peacetime security as well as lack of confidence in its capability to deal with the challenges contribute most to some misperceptions and discussions like safeguarding oil tankers with naval forces and building pipelines or railroads to bypass Malacca Straits and other choke points. Unfortunately, some perceptions of western analysts are just based on these misperceptions.

According to some western analysts, the Chinese are reinforcing their navy, concerned about the insecurity of the maritime routes, on which almost all of China's energy imports travel. The Chinese government's three pronged strategy to overcome 'Malacca dilemma' is investment, diplomacy and naval expansion (Zubir, Mokhzani 2006). At the same time, the so-called Chinese "String-of-Pearls Strategy" has become very popular among some western analysts.

Actually, most discussions on the 'Malacca dilemma' in China are among the academics and in the media. There are no signs or evidences showing that expansion of naval forces to safeguard the security of the sea lines has already been promoted as a part of the national energy security strategy or policy. Also, China's naval forces could not achieve the goal of safeguarding the oil tankers, even if China worked single-mindedly towards building its naval forces. Just as Carpenter (the author of *America's Coming War with China*) said, "It will not be a threat to the US unless China has a very large modern and capable navy which it has not remotely done to this point" (Massoud, Adla, 2006).

With increased concern about SLOC security, China is paying more and more attention to international cooperation while improving its energy transportation infrastructure and diversifying energy imports. On September 7, 2005, Ju Chengzhi, the head of China Maritime Administration, officially expressed Beijing's willingness to take active part in relevant cooperation for maintaining and strengthening sea lane security.[1] The growing concern about SLOC security provides opportunity and feasibility for Northeast Asian countries to cooperate on safeguarding the SLOC. But at the same time, some misperceptions and misunderstandings on

---

[1] *See* "Speeches of Ju Chengzhi, Head of the China Maritime Administration, on the Jakarta Conference on Malacca and Singaporean Straits Security," September 2005, at http://www.zgsyb.com/Article/ArticleShow.asp?ArticleID=9900

China or by the Chinese, also pose challenges to the cooperation.

To improve mutual trust and to further the cooperation, bilateral or multilateral strategic dialogue is very important. There are also some factors affecting SLOC security cooperation. These include the unstable political relationship among regional countries, different interpretations over security of the SLOC and the island's sovereignty disputes as well as overlapping maritime jurisdictional claims. Regarding the Malacca dilemma, some major powers are very much concerned about the impact of China's possible naval build-up on sea lane security and stability in East Asia. China also has similar worries from other powers. A section of Chinese analysts pay more attention to the impact of a possible security alliance between the United States, Japan, India and Australia on China's energy supply security or national security. In this regard, there is needs for close interaction among all the players, at the official as well as at the academic level.

Improving the regional energy transportation system is crucial to minimise the dependence on the Malacca Straits and other choke points and to increase capabilities to deal with possible disruptions. Lack of pipelines and other infrastructure has affected the development of the regional energy market and use of clean energy like natural gas. In the last couple of decades, a number of pipeline projects have been on the anvil, aiming to maximise the proposed energy cooperation with Russia, it has not been able to make any substantial progress so far. So we should work together to push forward the building of pipelines and other energy infrastructure (including the electricity power grids) and should strengthen the regional energy connections (like establishing an agreed legal and institutional framework to improve the climate for investment in non-renewable and renewable energy), while improving the domestic energy transportation system.

In order to strengthen cooperation on anti-piracy, anti-terrorism, prevention of traffic accidents, the following recommendations can be made: First, there is a need to have more governmental or academic communication or dialogue with littoral states and the ASEAN. Second, provision of necessary funds, technology and equipment for littoral states is necessary to improve the shipping conditions and effectively deal with piracy and terrorism. Third, exchange of information between the IOC and the information centres on piracy established by the littoral states, would be an important step towards ending the scourge of piracy and terrorism.

Lastly, it is necessary to explore the possibility of alternative sea lane routes besides the Malacca Straits. The Strait of Malacca is narrow; in terms of climate and geology, due to the equatorial calm zone and sandy flat sea floor, it guarantees a smooth voyage for tankers lighter than 100,000 tons. Heavier tankers still need to sail through the Sunda Strait. So, the improvement of shipping conditions in Sunda and Lombok Straits is very important for the increased passage of oil and LNG tankers in Northeast Asia in the coming years.

Bibliographical References

Special Report: Chinese Companies abroad (2005), 'The Dragon Tucks in,' *The Economist*, July 2, 2005, p. 61.

Council of Foreign Relations Report on the US – China Relationship, 'US-China Relations: An Affirmative Agenda', http://www.cfr.org/content/publications/attachments/ChinaTaskForce.pdf.

Juyan, Zhang (2004) 'American Think-tanks focus on China's oil issue', *Washingtongobserver*, April 14th 2004.

http://washingtonobserver.org.

Peter Van, Doren, Jerry Taylor 'Time to lay 1973 oil embargo to rest', http://www.cato.org/dailys/10-17-03-2.html

Abhyankar, Jarant, 'Piracy and Maritime Violence: A continuing threat to Maritime Industry"

http://www.itopf.com/abhyankar.pdf.

Harris, Stuart (2007), 'Changing Security Priorities: Toward an Integrated Dialouge on Resource Security', Paper to seminar 'Sino-Australian Security Relations: Regional Cooperation in an Interdependent World', Canberra, October 25-26, 2007

'Global Piracy Watch: Optimism as Piracy attacks fall for Third Year in a Row', http:www.Cargosecurity international.com.

Harris, Stuart (2007), 'Changing Security Priorities: Toward an Integrated Dialouge on Resource Security', Paper to seminar 'Sino-Australian Security Relations: Regional Cooperation in an Interdependent World', Canberra, October 25-26, 2007

Zubir, Mokhzani (2006) 'China's Energy Diplomacy in the Mekong River', Maritime Institute of Malaysia Online, May 2006

Massoud, Adla (2006), 'Oil May Fuel Sino-US Conflict', June 2006

8

Australian Energy Security: The benefits of self-sufficiency

ANDREW FORBES•

Australia's energy security is based on the assumption that its access to energy resources is secure: through an abundance of domestic energy resources and the ability to continue to import energy resources as required (Department of the Prime Minister and Cabinet, 2004). To maintain energy security, the Australian Government adopts many domestic measures to improve the efficiency of its energy industry. It also encourages explorations, predominantly in its exclusive economic zone for additional liquid energy resources. Australia's energy policy does not consider the potential impacts of disruption in the energy import and export on its economy.

• Visiting Senior Fellow, Australian National Centre for Ocean Resources and Security, University of Wollongong, Australia. These are the author's personal views and do not necessarily represent those of any institution with which he is associated.

This paper examines some of these issues, but does not consider issues associated with climate change as Australian policy on this topic is under development. First, this paper outlines Australia's energy production and current consumption. Second, it outlines Australia's energy trade to highlight the nexus between countries for economic, energy and national security. Third, it outlines security issues associated with protecting Australia's offshore energy infrastructure, its energy and global energy trades. It concludes with ideas on how navies might cooperate to protect seaborne trade.

8.1 Australia's Energy Production and Consumption

Australia is generally self-sufficient in energy resources particularly coal, gas and oil (Department of the Prime Minister and Cabinet, 2004). Energy consumption is dominated by electricity generation, transportation and manufacturing i.e 80 per cent of total consumption (Australian Bureau of Agricultural and Resource Economics, 2005). Coal accounts for 42 per cent of total primary energy consumption and contributes 81 per cent of the fuel for electricity generation. Oil accounts for 34 per cent of primary energy consumption and contributes 98 per cent of the fuel mix for the transportation sector. Natural gas accounts for 20 per cent of primary energy consumption (Australian Bureau of Agricultural and Resource Economics, 2005). Renewable energy accounts for only 5 per cent of total energy consumption and is not considered further in this paper (Australian Bureau of Agricultural and Resource Economics, 2005). The major problem Australia faces is that except coal, the majority of energy resources are found in remote locations, incurring significant distribution costs (Department of the Prime Minister and Cabinet, 2004).

8.1.1 Coal

Black coal is found in all Australian states, with the maximum deposits in New South Wales (NSW) and Queensland (41 and 57 per cent respectively). The holdings in Western

Australia (WA), South Australia (SA) and Tasmania are less but are important for local use. Only 25 per cent of black coal is consumed domestically, the remaining 75 per cent is exported. Australia's total brown coal is found in Victoria, with deposits also located in SA, WA, Tasmania and Victoria (Australian Bureau of Agricultural and Resource Economics, 2005). Brown coal mined in SA and Victoria is used for electricity generation (Australian Bureau of Agricultural and Resource Economics, 2005).

8.1.2 Uranium

Australia has 38 per cent of the world's low cost reserves of uranium. Uranium is obtained from three mines: Ranger in the Northern Territory, Olympic Dam (containing 70 per cent of known reserves) and Beverly, both in South Australia (Department of the Prime Minister and Cabinet, 2006). A fourth mine, Honeysuckle in SA, is expected to come on-line in 2008. Australia lacks a domestic nuclear industry. However, the Australian Nuclear Science and Technology Organisation conducts national nuclear research through OPAL reactor located at Lucas Heights in Sydney. It supplies radiopharmaceuticals, radioisotopes and neutron beams that are used in medical, environmental and industrial scientific research (Australian National Science and Technology Organisation).

8.1.3 Liquid Fuels

Australia is about 53 per cent self-sufficient in crude oil and natural gas liquid product, which is of the light variety and relatively low in sulphur (Australian Bureau of Agricultural and Resource Economics, 2007).

Australia is significantly dependent on offshore oil and gas supplies. It first discovered oil and gas fields in the offshore Gippsland basin in 1963 and started production in 1969. The Barrow Island oilfield in the Carnarvon Basin was discovered in 1964 and started production in 1967. Major gas fields were discovered in 1971 off North West Australia and started production in 1984. Oil and gas were also discovered in the Bonaparte Basin in the Timor Gap, between East Timor and Australia (Department of Industry, Science and Resources, 2001).

Currently, the Carnarvon Basin accounts for 63 per cent of crude oil, condensate and LPG production. The Gippsland Basin accounts for 19 per cent of petroleum liquid production. Additional crude oil and condensate comes from the onshore Cooper-Eromanga Basin. The substantial part of production from the Carnarvon Basin is exported, while the Gippsland Basin production is used in local refineries (Australian Bureau of Agricultural and Resource Economics, 2005). Significantly, much of Australia's offshore area is unexplored but is expected to contain additional oil and gas reserves (Department of the Prime Minister and Cabinet, 2004).

In 2005-06 the Carnarvon Basin produced 66 per cent of Australia's natural gas, with 13 per cent coming from the Cooper-Eromanga Basin and 19 per cent from the Gippsland Basin (Australian Bureau of Agricultural and Resource Economics, 2005). The Gippsland and Cooper-Eromanga Basins supply 90 per cent of the domestic gas market for SA, Victoria, NSW (New South Wales) and Queensland; while the Carnarvon Basin supplies to WA gas market, but exports the majority of its product (Australian Bureau of Agricultural and Resource Economics, 2005). Australia has signed contracts to supply LNG to Asian markets such as the recent $25 billion contract with China (Department of the Prime Minister and Cabinet, 2004). There is a growing commercial use of coal seam gas from black coal deposits in Queensland and NSW, feeding the Brisbane and Sydney gas markets (Australian Bureau of Agricultural and Resource Economics, 2007).

8.1.4 Transportation energy

Transportation accounts for 35 per cent of total energy consumption and is growing at 2.4 per cent per annum. In 2006–07 around 87 per cent of the products from Australia's eight refineries were automotive gasoline, diesel fuel and aviation turbine fuel. Australia is less self-sufficient in the heavier products, such as kerosene, diesel, fuel oil and lubricants (Australian Bureau of Agricultural and Resource Economics, 2007).

8.1.5 Electricity Generation

In 2004–05, black coal accounted for 56 per cent of electricity generation, brown coal 21 per cent, gas 14.3 per cent, hydro 6.4 per cent and oil 1.4 per cent. By 2029-30 the share of electricity generation will be 50.8 per cent from black coal, 22.6 per cent from gas, 17.7 per cent from brown coal, 4.5 per cent from hydro and 0.9 per cent from oil (Department of the Prime Minister and Cabinet, 2004). A recent study estimated that nuclear power would be 20–50 per cent more costly to produce than current coal-fired plants (Department of the Prime Minister and Cabinet). A key focus of Australia's energy policy is to improve the generation and distribution of electricity to consumers. The electricity industry was restructured in the early 1990s, with the State owned utilities vertically disaggregated into separate generation, transmission, distribution and retail supply components (Australian Bureau of Agricultural and Resource Economics, 2005). Use of clean coal technology for electricity generation requires heavy investment. This is the real focus of Australian energy policies.

8.1.6 Disruptions to energy supplies

Australia has experienced major supply disruptions which affected Australian economy. In September 1998 there was an explosion and fire at Esso gas plant in Longford, Victoria which killed two people, injured eight, and stopped gas supplies throughout the state affecting four million people. The economic cost of no gas supplies for 19 days was assessed at $1.3 billion (M Peters, P Aitken, J Mitchell and M Northcott). In September and October 2003, there were serious disruptions to aviation fuel supplies to Sydney Airport which led to rationing of fuel for aircraft until additional fuel could be delivered. In June 2008, an explosion at the natural gas facility on Varanus Island off Western Australia caused 30 per cent reduction in gas supplies to the state, adversely impacting business, agriculture and households. The key focus of Australia's energy policy is to ensure reliable, competitively priced supplies of energy (Department of the Prime Minister and Cabinet, 2004). To this end, Australia holds about 50 days' supply of crude oil and product, as it takes about 25 days for crude oil to be sourced from Singapore (Department of the Prime Minister and Cabinet, 2004).

8.2 Australia's Energy Trade

Australia is a significant energy exporter. Since 1986 it has been the world's largest coal exporter and from 1989 it emerged as one of the largest LNG and uranium exporters. Australia produces light, sweet crude oil and oil reserves are located in the north and north-west which attracts a high premium on export markets (Department of the Prime Minister and Cabinet, 2004). The value of Australia's energy exports in 2006-07 was about $38 billion. However, some energy resources are imported, either due to a lack of domestic resources or more usually, because it is cheaper to import product than transport energy supplies around Australia. This is particularly the case for northern Australia where it is often cheaper to import refined fuel from Asia, predominantly Singapore, than to supply it from refineries in south east Australia. Energy imports in 2006-07 were about $22 billion (Australian Bureau of Agricultural and Resource Economics, 2007).

8.2.1 Coal Exports

Australia accounts for about 7 per cent of world black coal production. Black coal is of high bituminous quality with low sulphur and ash content (Australian Bureau of Agricultural and Resource Economics, 2005). Australia has about a third of the black coal trade and nearly two-thirds of the metallurgical coal trade. NSW is the major supplier of thermal coal exports and Queensland is the major supplier of metallurgical coal exports. The major bottleneck to continuing exports is the ability to load coal onto ships and currently there is a huge backlog of ships waiting outside NSW and Queensland ports to take on coal. In 2006-07, Australia exported 131.92 million tonnes (Mt) of metallurgical coal, with Japan receiving 48.91Mt, the EU 24.85Mt, India 19.56Mt, Taiwan 8.03Mt, South Korea 6.25Mt, and China 2.97Mt. Similarly 111.68 million tonnes of thermal coal were also exported, with Japan receiving 58.65Mt, South Korea 15.06Mt, Taiwan 16.23Mt, China 3.22Mt, Malaysia 3.54Mt, other ASEAN 3.68Mt and India 0.72Mt (Australian Bureau of Agricultural and Resource Economics, 2007).

8.2.2 Liquid Fuel Exports

In 2006-07 Australia exported 15963 million litres (ML) of crude oil and other refinery feedstock. Singapore received 3751ML, South Korea 3873ML, Japan 1957ML, China 518ML and Taiwan 446ML. 2842ML of LPG was exported with Japan receiving 1821ML, China 308ML and South Korea 384ML. 1762ML of refined products were also exported with Singapore receiving 576ML, New Zealand 872ML other Pacific countries 131ML, Japan 84ML and Fiji 4ML (Australian Bureau of Agricultural and Resource Economics, 2007). 15.2 million tonnes of LNG were also exported but recipient countries are not recorded in published Australian statistics (Australian Bureau of Agricultural and Resource Economics, 2007). In 2007, according to British Petroleum, Australia exported 20.24 billion cubic metres (bcm) of natural gas, 16.05 bcm to Japan, 3.30 bcm to China, 0.56 bcm to South Korea and 0.33bcm to Taiwan (BP Statistical Review of World Energy, 2008).

8.2.3 Liquid Fuel Imports

In 2006-07 Australia imported 25341 million litres (ML) of crude oil and other refinery feedstock. Of the total import 6710ML was imported from Vietnam, 3716ML from Malaysia, 3391ML from Indonesia, 3236ML from the Middle East, 2059ML from Papua New Guinea, and 846ML from

Singapore. 18268ML of refined products were also imported, with 7666ML imported from Singapore, 818ML from South Korea, 642ML from the Middle East, 8ML from Malaysia and 17ML from Indonesia (Australian Bureau of Agricultural and Resource Economics, 2007). Australia also imports natural gas from the Bonaparte Basin in the Timor Sea to supply the Northern Territory market (Australian Bureau of Agricultural and Resource Economics, 2005).

8.2.4 Uranium Exports

In 2005, Australia exported 12360 tonnes of uranium, valued at $573 million to 10 countries, including the United States (36 per cent), France (11 per cent), Japan (22 per cent) and South Korea (9 per cent). Australia has a tight regulatory regime for uranium mining industry. Australia also abides by all international treaties and conventions concerning the transportation of uranium Spent fuel from the ANSTO reactor at Lucas Heights in Sydney is shipped to France for processing (Department of Foreign Affairs and Trade).

8.3 Australia's Energy Security Issues

In order to maintain energy security, Australia has three concerns:

1. Security of offshore energy infrastructure,
2. Protection of Australian seaborne energy flows,
3. Protection of global energy flows.

8.3.1 Australia's Offshore Energy Infrastructure

The September 2001 terrorist attacks in the United States led to a fundamental reassessment of the security vulnerabilities of the maritime transportation industry. Amended *International Convention for the Safety of Life at Sea, 1974,* and the *International Ship and Port Facility Security (ISPS) Code* was introduced. On 12 December 2003, the Maritime Transport Security Act (MTSA) 2003 was passed and came into force on 1 July 2004.

Concurrently, a Taskforce on Offshore Maritime Security had been examining the security arrangements for offshore oil and gas facilities. On 15 December 2004, the Australian Prime Minister announced that the Government would assume responsibility for all offshore counter-terrorism activity and the protection of the offshore oil and gas facilities. To achieve this, an additional two *Armidale* class patrol boats were to be purchased for the Royal Australian Navy to undertake patrols in the North West Shelf (location of the Carnarvon Basin) and in the Timor Sea. Flowing from the work of the Taskforce, the MTSA was amended in June 2005 to extend Australia's maritime security regime to Australia's offshore oil and gas facilities, resulting in the MTSA being renamed (MTOFSA) (Maritime Transport and Offshore Facilities Security Act 2003.

In order to respond to any threat to the oil and gas facilities, a program of augmented security patrols was instituted to increase the level of security within the patrol areas to deter those who might contemplate or plan an attack on these assets. The benefit of augmented security patrolling is its apparent unpredictable timing and location, and thus its ability to shape the behaviour of the crews of vessels in the vicinity of offshore platforms. The pulsing technique, by focusing patrol assets on specific targets for a defined and limited period of time, substantially reduces costs as compared to providing blanket air and surface coverage.

8.3.2 Protecting Australia's seaborne energy flows

Australia's trade vulnerability is recognised in its defence policy. The Australian Defence Force (ADF) is assigned for the protection of shipping. It reroutes ships away from threat areas, and to convoy those priority ships that cannot be rerouted using the Royal Australian Navy's (RAN) surface combatants with air cover, noting range and endurance considerations. If supplies were disrupted by military or terrorist action, navy would respond appropriately, with an option of convoying these ships.

A bulk coal carrier would be subjected to military or terrorist action, although a liquid tanker would be a more viable proposition. Certainly for the newly constituted LNG supply to China, these cargoes might be considered significant, requiring a naval escort. All Australian-Asian trade passes through Southeast Asia, either to the ASEAN states or to North Asia. The majority of Australian export trade to Japan transits the Indonesian Archipelago, passing through the Lombok Strait, then the Strait of Makassar into the Pacific Ocean, south of the Philippine Archipelago. An alternative route is the Ombai-Wetar Strait, then going through either the Makassar Strait or the Molucca Passage. Japanese imports are routed east of Papua New Guinea. Trade going to the north west of Australia can transit part of the Makassar or Karimata Straits before passing through the Malacca Strait. The Sunda Strait can also be used as an alternative to the Lombok Strait, but it is a less direct route and is beset by difficulties.

More specifically, Australia's exports of crude petroleum and oil transit through the Lombok and Makassar Straits, and then via the South China Sea if bound for Hong Kong or China, or via the Philippines Sea if bound for Korea and Japan. Exports of coke and coal transit through the Lombok and Malacca Straits if bound for Burma and Europe, or they transit through the Lombok and Makassar Straits and then the Philippines Sea if destined for Hong Kong, Taiwan, Korea and Japan. The LNG trade leaves North-West Australia through the Suva Sea, Ombai Strait, Manipa Strait, and east of Obi Island through the Moluccan Passage and hence direct to China and Japan. Thus continued access to the sea lanes in the Indonesian archipelago is critical for Australian trade.

8.3.2 Protecting global energy flows

Australia relies upon overseas trade for her economic survival, with China, Japan, South Korea and Taiwan being major Australian trading partners. The Asia-Pacific and the North Asia are the most economically dynamic regions in the world and are based predominantly on seaborne trade. It relies on energy imports from the Middle East to fuel economic growth. The Middle East supplies about 50 per cent of China's oil requirements, about 85 per cent of Japan's and about 50 per cent of South Korea's. Thus oil tankers passing through it would require protection in the event of hostilities.

8.4 Regional Naval Cooperation

As the majority of energy-flows in Asia are seaborne in nature, navies would be involved in the protection of this shipping if it were threatened. In 1951, the Radford-Collins Naval Control of Shipping Agreement was signed among the US, UK, Australia and New Zealand aiming to protect merchant shipping and ASW operations during the periods of tension or war. It delineated national areas of responsibility for naval control of shipping, local defence and anti-submarine warfare in the Indian and southern Pacific Oceans. Under the agreement, the parties periodically hold exercises to test and assess common procedures, and usually take the form of NCS command post exercises.

Apart from the Radford-Collins Agreement there are also international naval trade protection fora known as Shipping Working Groups (SWG) like NATO and the Pacific and Indian Oceans (PACIO SWG). The members of the PACIO group are the US, UK, Republic of Korea, Australia and Chile, Singapore. South Africa has observer status. Their effort is to develop common strategic and operational level concepts and to test communications links annually.

Conclusion

How can countries and their navies work together to protect shipping?

Identification of common shipping threats of countries is the prerequisite to reach on agreement among these countries for protection. From this flows the identificatior. of possible responses to the common threat, leading to assistance in developing relevant capabilities if required. This is perhaps the most critical issue, as there is no apparent general agreement on a common maritime threat assessment for shipping in the Asia-Pacific region. Some form of common agreement between countries should progressively lead to cooperation between agencies, then bilateral and eventually multilateral naval cooperation. Interoperability is difficult to achieve but the harmonisation of procedures is a useful first step.

The key to maritime cooperation between navies is trust and understanding. Collaboration through multilateral activities provides an understanding of how each navy thinks, operates and what capabilities it possesses. It also provides an opportunity for personnel to interact, exchange ideas and professional expertise and gain an understanding of each other. Competency building through specific activities allows navies to train together to further enhance their skills. Cooperation and capacity building allow more experienced navies to pass on knowledge and expertise to other members. Importantly, 'experience' is not limited to larger navies; rather it is based on specific skill sets across a range of navies.

In each region a number of countries have a natural claim to involvement in the protection of shipping transiting through their region. This is then somewhat complicated by the presence of major powers who may also intervene to protect their own national interests.

The most suitable framework for the protection of shipping in the Asia-Pacific region might be the adoption of NATO NCS standards. While it would not be possible to reach the political agreement and military integration of NATO forces, adoption of their standards would assist the Asia-Pacific as the doctrine, administration framework and training requirements already exist. They would necessarily be modified to suit the Asia-Pacific political, geographic and military capability requirements.

Bibliographical References

Department of the Prime Minister and Cabinet (2004), *Securing Australia's Energy Future*, Canberra, p. 20.

Department of Prime Minister and Cabinet (2004), *Securing Australia's Energy Future*, p. 5.

Australian Bureau of Agricultural and Resource Economics (2005), *Energy in Australia 2006*, Canberra, 2007, p. 57.

Australian Bureau of Agricultural and Resource Economics (2005), *Australian Energy: national and state projections to 2029-30*, Canberra, p. 26.

Australian Bureau of Agricultural and Resource Economics (2005), *Energy in Australia 2006*, p. 69.

Department of the Prime Minister and Cabinet (2004), *Securing Australia's Energy Future*, p. 6.

Australian Bureau of Agricultural and Resource Economics (2005), *Energy in Australia 2006*, p. 5.

Australian Bureau of Agricultural and Resource Economics (2005), *Energy in Australia 2006*, p. 11.

Department of the Prime Minister and Cabinet (2006), *Uranium Mining, Processing and Nuclear Energy Review*, Canberra, pp. 3, 21–22.

Australian National Science and Technology Organisation, *About ANSTO*, www.ansto.gov.au.

Australian Bureau of Agricultural and Resource Economics (2007), *Energy in Australia 2008*, Canberra, p. 15.

Department of Industry, Science and Resources (2001), *Hydrocarbon Basins of Australia*, www.isr.gov.au/resources/petr_exploration/2001/Web_basins_01.pdf

Australian Bureau of Agricultural and Resource Economics (2006), *Energy in Australia 2006*, pp. 21, 23; Australian Bureau of Agricultural and Resource Economics (2008), *Energy in Australia 2008*, p. 15.

Department of the Prime Minister and Cabinet (2004), *Securing Australia's Energy Future*, p. 9.

Australian Bureau of Agricultural and Resource Economics (2006), *Energy in Australia 2006*, p. 35.

Australian Bureau of Agricultural and Resource Economics (2006), *Energy in Australia 2006*, p. 37.

Department of Prime Minister and Cabinet (2004), *Securing Australia's Energy Future*, p 62.

Australian Bureau of Agricultural and Resource Economics (2007), *Energy in Australia 2008*, p. 5.

Australian Bureau of Agricultural and Resource Economics (2007), *Energy in Australia 2008*, pp. 25, 71.

Australian Bureau of Agricultural and Resource Economics (2005), *Energy in Australia 2006*, p. 45.

Department of the Prime Minister and Cabinet, *Uranium Mining, Processing and Nuclear Energy Review*, p. 2.

Australian Bureau of Agricultural and Resource Economics (2005), *Energy in Australia 2006*, p. 45.

M Peters, P Aitken, J Mitchell and M Northcott, *Esso Gas Plant Explosion*, www.members.iinet.au/~jinsploj/pdf/longford.pdf

Department of Prime Minister and Cabinet (2004), *Securing Australia's Energy Future*, p. 116.

Department of Prime Minister and Cabinet (2004), *Securing Australia's Energy Future*, pp. 1124–125.

Department of Prime Minister and Cabinet (2004), *Securing Australia's Energy Future*, p 118.

Australian Bureau of Agricultural and Resource Economics (2007), *Energy in Australia 2008*, p. 2.

Australian Bureau of Agricultural and Resource Economics (2005), *Energy in Australia 2006*, pp. 2–3.

Australian Bureau of Agricultural and Resource Economics (2007), *Energy in Australia 2008*, p. 13.

Australian Bureau of Agricultural and Resource Economics (2007), *Energy in Australia 2008*, p. 21.

BP Statistical Review of World Energy (2008), London, p. 30.

Australian Bureau of Agricultural and Resource Economics (2007), *Energy in Australia 2008*, p. 23.

Australian Bureau of Agricultural and Resource Economics (2005), *Energy in Australia 2006*, p. 37.

Department of Foreign Affairs and Trade, *Nuclear Safety and Transport*, www.dfat.gov.au/security/safety_nuc_shipment.html

Department of Foreign Affairs and Trade, *Transport of spent fuel from Australia to France*, www.dfat.gov.au/security/safety_nuc_shipment.html

Maritime Transport and Offshore Facilities Security Act 2003, at http://comlaw.gov.au/ComLaw/Legislation/ActCompilation

1.nsf/0/F8311AC193742AF6CA257084001F6DB0/$file/MaritimeTransOffshoreFacil Security2003_WD02.pdf, (21 November 2005).

9

Europe Debates its Energy Security: Any lessons for Asia?

Michal Meidan

Energy Security has been troubling States since the dawn of industrialization. Mastering coal for military and civilian transport, growing reliance on oil and gas for industry and residential use: the need for available, affordable and sustainable energy has preoccupied decision-makers for decades and centuries[1]. But only when resources were deemed finite, and a cause for conflict, did energy security become an issue of international concern as well as a question of domestic politics.

The current European vision of energy security, that gained ground after the oil crises and the creation of the International Energy Agency in the 1970s, places markets at

[1] *See* J.-M Chevalier (2004), *Les Grandes Batailles de l'énergie*, Paris : Gallimard ; Michael T. Klare (2001), *Resource Wars : The New Landscape of Global Conflict*, London: Macmillan

the forefront of energy interactions. In the context of the common market, cooperative measures were part of the reconciliation process that brought states together, and the premises for regional integration. Moreover, with relatively stable oil prices throughout the 1980s and until the turn of the century, the "market approach" paradigm seemed an adequate response to the risks to energy security.

In recent years, rising oil and gas prices, increasing political instability in the Middle East and Africa and the emergence of producer and consumer countries with new approaches to energy security have challenged conventional thinking in Europe and have triggered renewed debate on its approach to energy security.

This chapter will therefore address the following questions: what were the underlying principles that guided the integration of the European energy market and European energy policies? What are the new challenges facing Europe and how have they shaped the continent's evolving approach to its energy security? How is this relevant to Asia and what are the implications for future cooperation between Asia and Europe?

In order to answer these questions, the chapter is organized as follows: the first section will provide an overview of the rationale that has guided the European energy policies and assess its achievements and shortcomings in safeguarding the continents' energy security. The second part will look at the reassessment taking place in Europe since the emergence of China and India as major "strategic" consumers and of Russia as a producer willing to use energy for political leverage, with the latter providing, arguably, the greatest cause for debate in Europe. The chapter will conclude with an assessment of the relevance of the European experience and its paradigms for Asia.

9.1 The European Union's energy policy: Market rationale

European definitions of energy security are closely related to the history, economic structure and consumption patterns in these countries. While discrepancies remain between the individual member States and the EU institutions[2], and the EU's energy policy remains in the making, common paradigms underlie the energy strategies of EU member states which allow a certain consensus in the Union as a whole.

Apart from the European Coal and Steel Community (ECSC) and the European Atomic Energy community (Euratom, discussed below), energy policy has been one of the weaker components of European integration. Energy paradigms have nevertheless, been defined by three general perspectives: First, attempts to consolidate a competitive internal market; second, the desire to formulate a common environmental policy with fiscal measures as key instruments and third, the European Energy Charter and the Charter Treaty which were aimed at creating international market regimes capable of securing the EU's energy supplies from its Eastern neighbours (Andersen, Svein S, 2000). The EU's first Energy White paper thus stated that "Market integration is the central determining factor in the Community's energy policy"(Europa,1995) and against the backdrop of different national energy policies, it further stated that "a Community energy policy framework in which Member States are working towards agreed common objectives would enable the Community to respond effectively to the destabilizing effects of changes in energy prices" (Europa, 1995).

The emphasis is therefore on the market's role as a regulator of supply and demand. Strategies aim to ensure that natural resources are provided to citizens at economically viable conditions. In terms of external challenges to energy security, this first White Paper asserts that security of supply will be achieved through "effective internal policy corrections to market rules, by encouraging fuel diversification, by enlarging choices with the promotion of energy efficiency, renewables ..." (Europa, 1995).

---

2 As pipeline projects in Europe have shown, with the Nabucco pipeline failing to emerge and the Blue-Stream pipeline creating increasing controversy.

This approach stems from two main factors, the first being the European Union's *raison d'être* as mentioned above, the second from global liberalization trends in the 1980s and 1990s which seemed valid and efficient until the turn of the century. Indeed, one of the first undertakings of the European Community (later to become the European Union) was the creation of a common market for coal and steel, needed for Europe's reconstruction after World War II. Despite its relative failure in economic terms, the ECSC was an important symbol of using economic tools to promote the political goal of reunification and long term stability (Andrews-Speed, Philip 2004). As a stepping stone to further deeper integration, the ECSC embodied the above mentioned principles and the political will of member States. The rationale of increased liberalization of energy transactions gained ground after 1970s oil shocks, which also led to the creation of the International Energy Agency (IEA). Substitution, increased energy efficiency and shifting to service oriented economies were the responses in developed countries. In Europe, consolidating Internal Energy Market in order to raise the Union's economic competitiveness was seen as the way to enhance energy security. And in a sense, until the turn of the century, supply security was low on the list of threats as supply flowed in relatively cheap prices, uninterrupted onto the continent. The focus of energy policies in the EU was on integrating energy markets, enhancing and securing physical interconnectivity (Frizton et al. 2007), as well as achieving a more environmentally friendly growth path (with the ensuing debate on the importance of nuclear energy) (The Economist, 2007).

9.2 Europe rethinks its energy policy

The market approach and the liberal rationale were challenged by a number of key events at the turn of the century. The Californian energy crisis in 2000 drew attention to the risks of liberalization, which also found an echo in the debate on the merits of deregulation (Buchan, David, 2002). The September 11 attacks and the ensuing turmoil in the

Middle East contributed to redefining threat perceptions, highlighting once again the physical threats to energy infrastructures and their effect on prices. The rising prices due to the surging demand from developing countries, (especially China and India) and uncertainties over the future of Venezuela's energy sector led to the top policy priorities for supply security.

Furthermore, the American-led invasion of Iraq and the assessment by some that it was for domination of the country's natural resources, the emergence of Russia as a strong producer country that fully uses its energy resources as a political tool, recentralized into the hands of the President (L. Buszynski, 2006), seemed to herald a new era in which supplies could no longer be left to the markets.

In 2002 the English House of Lords noted that "markets on their own cannot cope with the geopolitical problems that are the main source of security concerns" (A. Maurer, O. Geden, C. Marcelis, 2006), and after the oil skirmish between Russia and Ukraine in January 2006, a response to "adverse influence on market fundamentals" (Europa, 2006 b) became urgent. Thus, the subsequent EU paper on energy policy defined "Increasing dependence on imports from unstable regions and suppliers" as "a serious risk". Coupled with the facts that "some major producers and consumers have been using energy as a political lever" and with the emergence "of external actors not playing by the same market rules nor being subject to the same competitive pressures domestically, the development of a coherent and focused external EU energy policy, drawing on the full range of EU internal and external policies, would enhance the collective external energy security of the Union."

Energy geopolitics and rising oil prices highlighted the EU's vulnerability and its dependence on its Eastern neighbour, now deemed unreliable. In 2004, total EU-27 energy supply reached 1800 million tons oil equivalent (mtoe), a little lower than in the US where supply totaled

2340 mtoe[3]. Supply was largely dominated by oil and gas which accounted for nearly 60 per cent (36 per cent and 24 per cent respectively), with nuclear and renewable energy representing an additional 21 per cent. However, only a small share of this supply comes from indigenous European sources (37 per cent of natural gas and 18 per cent of oil in 2004 were from European production) (Europa, 2007b), and in the future, Europe will remain dependent on external sources of energy, especially oil and gas.

Currently, almost half of Europe's oil imports come from the Former Soviet Union, and a quarter of its gas crosses over by pipeline. Despite efforts to diversify import sources, Russia is slated to remain Europe's most important provider of oil and gas. Arguably, it is not the dependency itself that is so worrisome for European capitals, rather Russia's recent pipeline politics that have heightened the sense of insecurity (Bilefsky, Danand and Judy Dempsey, 2007). Nevertheless, one must not forget that for producer countries, ensuring an outlet for their exports is just as important as securing supplies are for an importing country. The pipelines tying Europe to Russia create interdependence between the two. Furthermore, despite the expansion of Russian exports to Europe, its share in European imports has dropped from roughly 80 per cent in 1980 to around 40 per cent currently. Since 1990, 80 per cent of the rise in EU gas imports has been from non-Russian sources (Noel, Pierre, 2008),

---

3 Figures for China and the US are cited from the BP (2007), *BP Statistical Review 2007*. European figures are from Europa (2006a) *Commission of the European Communities, Green Paper: a European strategy for sustainable, competitive and secure energy*, COM (2006) 105 final, http://ec.europa.eu/energy/green-paper-energy/doc/2006_03_08_gp_document_en.pdf, accessed on January 17, 2008. There is little discrepancy however between the figures for Europe cited in the BP Statistical Review and in the EU Commission paper.

Till recently, diplomatically the EU has been facing the problem of having a unified energy security approach. As per the EU documents, the major source of uncertainty surrounds "the ability and willingness of major oil and gas producers to step up investment in order to meet rising global demand" (IEA, 2006) which implies that policies envision a supply crunch due to underinvestment and not due to political manoeuvring or denied physical access to resources by the producer or a third state. "Locking up" oil is therefore not an option and the "concept of physical shortage is misleading and unhelpful. In a reasonably competitive market for a reasonably fungible commodity like oil, 'shortage' is manifested by higher prices rather than physical shortages" (J. Dunkerely, 2006). This is not the case for gas, which ties producers and consumers via pipelines.

Moreover, the EU Green paper emphasizes that "Well-functioning world markets are the best ways of ensuring safe and affordable energy supplies". The European Union has, however, designed a series of initiatives including dialouges with key producers and consumers, focusing on Russia, Central Asia and key regional bilateral partners in order to improve legal and regulatory frameworks in their energy sectors and to help integrate regional electricity markets. Dialogues with other consumers, (such as China, the US and Brazil) emphasize cooperation in low carbon energy technologies, increasing energy efficiency, and promoting the use of renewable energy (Europa, 2007c). The EU's energy policy is still in the making, and member states are working bilaterally with one another to ensure their energy security as they perceive it. This does not, however, invalidate the basic thinking and the existence of a common approach as embodied by the concepts stated above. In fact, there is a clear recognition that Europe stands to gain from a common approach (Godement, Francois, 2007).

Hence, EU energy policy priorities on the supply side focus on improving investment climates in producer countries.

A new trend has, however, emerged with the rise of new consumers and producers who seem to be playing by different rules.

9.3 Are there any lessons for Asia?

The European experience seems hardly capable of providing a workable blueprint for Asian integration. Differences in economic systems, development stages and most importantly political reconciliation mean that Asia will have to find its own path towards regionalization. Nevertheless, the European experience and paradigms that underlie it can be adapted and made useful to Asian realities.

Asia, despite its energy disparities between oil importers and exporters, is expected to remain dependent on the Middle East for next several decades. Widespread use of coal (especially in China and India) bodes ill for air pollution. If policies aren't revised, sulphur dioxide emissions in 2030 will be more than three times the 1990 level. In view of these challenges, the three fundamental principles (described above) that guided the EU could prove helpful: Attempts to consolidate competitive internal markets would, at the first stage, enhance energy efficiency within individual Asian countries and set the framework for a common basis for regional markets at a later stage; Second, common goals towards environmentally friendly development will allow developing countries to adopt a more sustainable development path. Ideally, Asia could cooperate on technology transfers, joint R&D, or even regulatory frameworks for adopting greener development paths, with support from the EU. Finally, dialogues along the lines of the Energy Charter Treaty could enhance mutual trust and lead to greater exchanges of information. This could also be achieved under the auspices of the IEA. By integrating China and India as observers or members, experience sharing on stockpiling as well as greater transparency through information sharing could provide solid building blocks for increased regional cooperation.

Infrastructure security is also a possible avenue for cooperation. It is, however, more appropriate to begin at the subregional level, as electricity grids in ASEAN countries are already partially connected, and pipeline projects across the continent are being envisaged. The building blocks of cooperation could therefore be negotiations on common technical attributes and standards that could later facilitate interconnecting physical infrastructure.

Whilst energy is still at the very core of national interests and is perceived as a strategic issue, most countries agree that regional and international cooperation on energy security is a necessary supplement to national initiatives. China's recently published White Paper on energy maintains that "Energy security is a global issue (….) which demands that the international community strengthen dialogue and cooperation to work out a solution together" (White Paper on Energy, 2007). India too is at a transitional point in defining its energy policy, and while it would ultimately like to achieve energy independence, rising demand and projections of increasing dependence on foreign sources of energy mean that it too will have to face the vagaries of Middle Eastern and African politics. Prominent Indian experts have called for greater action abroad, by cooperating more intensely in the international arena, and through "enlightened diplomacy and negotiations" (Madan, Tanvi, 2006).

This momentum should therefore be seized. As mentioned above, the EU path is not a blueprint for Asian integration but the underlying perceptions can be: functional cooperation on technical issues, a stronger push for gradual liberalization in order to achieve greater efficiency and dialogue to promote more environmentally friendly growth paths will prove beneficial for individual states and the region as a whole. Regional dialogue with producer states, along the lines of the ECT, could help Asian countries renegotiate their "Asian premium" on Middle East exports. The EU can — and should — contribute funding; technical and regulatory know-how as well as a candid assessment of the achievements and shortcomings of its attempts at a common energy policy. It is Asia, however, that will have to shore up the political will.

Bibliographical References

Andersen, Svein S. (2000), "European Integration and the Changing Paradigm of Energy Policy: The case of natural gas liberalisation", ARENA Working Papers WP 99/12, available at http://www.arena.uio.no/publications/wp00_13.htm (accessed on June 20, 2008)

Europa (1995), *An Energy Policy for the European Union* COM(95) 682 final, 1995

Andrews-Speed, Philip (2004), "A European Approach to Energy Security", *in* François Godement et. al. (eds), *Asia and Europe: Cooperating for Energy Security*, Paris: Centre asie IFRI.

Frizton et al. (2007), 'Protecting Europe's Critical Infrastructures: Problems and Prospects', Journal of Contingencies and Crisis Management, vol. 15 no. 1, March.

The Economist (2007), "Nuclear fallout", *The Economist*, August 2, 2007

Buchan, David (2002), "The Threat Within: Deregulation and Energy Security", *Survival*, vol. 44, no. 3, pp. 105-116

L. Buszynski (2006), 'Oil and territory in Putin's relations with China and Japan', *Pacific Review*, 19 (3), 287-303

A. Maurer, O. Geden, C. Marcelis, (2006), *Perspectives for the European Union's External Energy Policy: Discourse, Ideas and Interests in Germany, the UK, Poland and France*, Working Paper FG1 2006/ 17, (SWP, Berlin)

Europa (2006b), *An External Policy to Serve Europe's Energy Interests*, Paper from Commission/SG/HR for the European Council S160/06

Europa (2007b), EU Commission Staff Working Document, *EU Energy Policy Data* SEC (2007) 12, available at ec.europa.eu/ energy/energy_policy/doc/02_eu_energy_policy_data_en.pdf , accessed on January 15, 2007

Bilefsky, Danand and Judy Dempsey (2007), 'Merkel rebukes Russia', *International Herald Tribune*, 9 January; Stephen Castle, 'EU tries to turn 'Energy Weapon' against Gazprom', *International Herald Tribune*, 19 September 2007

Noel, Pierre (2008), 'Europe needs a single market for Natural Gas', *The Financial Times*, May 5

IEA (2006), *World Energy Outlook 2006,* (OECD/IEA, Paris)

J. Dunkerely (2006), 'Lessons from the past thirty years', *Energy Policy,* 24, 503-507

Europa (2007c), *Developing external energy policy for the EU,* MEMO/07/533, available at http://www.europa.eu/rapid/pressReleasesAction.do?reference=MEMO/07/533&format=HTML&aged=0&language=EN&guiLanguage=en accessed January 17, 2008

Godement, François (2007), "Energy security – different approaches » in Peter Ludlow, (ed.), *The EU and China,* The European Strategy Foundation, Ponte de Lima, pp. 72-91

White Paper on Energy (2007), available in English at http://www.china.org.cn/english/environment/236955.htm#8

Madan, Tanvi (2006). India, the Brookings Energy Series.

10

EU-Energy Policies and its Supply Security Strategies

DR FRANK UMBACH

The EU's March 2007 Decisions on Energy and Climate Protection Policies

In March 2007, the European Council had agreed on an integrated climate and energy policy with an 'Energy Action Plan' (EAP) for the next two years (2007–2009). The EU's long-term strategy for energy supply security needs to cope with uninterrupted physical availability of energy products in the market, at a price which is affordable for all private and industrial consumers. At the same time, the EU needs to balance its future energy supply policies with growing environmental concerns, which has become an even more important objective in the light of the Kyoto Protocol and the global debates of mitigating climate change. In this context, the EAP favours a liberalized internal market for gas and electricity, enhanced measures for security of supply and a common approach to an external energy policy with a global dimension. The summit's conclusions are mostly in line with the previous recommendations of the EU Commission in January 2007, its Green Book of 2006, and its 'Green Paper on Energy Efficiency' of September 2005. Energy policy is aimed at being a careful balance between all three parameters: security of supply, competitiveness and environmental sustainability.

Table 10.1 : EU - Primary Energy Demand 1971-2030 (Mtoe)

	1990	**2005**	**2015**	**2030**	**2005–2015***	**2005–2030***
Coal	451	317	291	275	-0.8 per cent	-0.6 per cent
Oil	626	671	678	670	0.1 per cent	-0.0 per cent
Gas	295	444	509	610	1.4 per cent	1.3 per cent
Nuclear	207	260	239	159	-0.8 per cent	-2.0 per cent
Hydro	25	26	34	37	2.8 per cent	1.4 per cent
Biomass and waste	46	83	127	182	4.3 per cent	3.2 per cent
Other renew-ables	3	13	33	72	10.0 per cent	7.2 per cent
Total	**1,653**	**1,814**	**1,910**	**2,006**	**0.5 per cent**	**0.4 per cent**

*Average annual rate of growth.

(Source: IEA, World Energy Outlook 7, Paris 2007, p. 616).

The German EU presidency negotiated the world's most comprehensive action plan (containing 17 individual measures) on climate protection and energy supply. The EU-27 was able to agree on a set of tasks and targets at the March summit of 2007 such as:

1. Energy efficiency should be increased by 20 per cent across the EU by 2020;
2. The goals of the Kyoto Protocol should be exceeded by reducing carbon emissions by 20 per cent till 2020 compared to 1990 (if other industrialized countries such as the USA, India and China commit themselves to similar policies, the EU would be willing to reduce emissions even by 30 per cent);
3. Additionally, a 20 per cent share of the energy mix should be generated from renewable energy sources by 2020. Latvia, Sweden, Finland and Austria have already attained this target, although the Swedish and Finnish success is due to the use of nuclear energy.

The European Commission's energy demand management strategy has always emphasized the diversification in energy supply, promotion of renewable energies and a neutral look at the nuclear option. After years of discrediting coal, the Commission also views coal now as an important energy source in the future which can contribute to enhance security of supply in the EU. It decided to support the development of clean coal technologies.

Table 10.2 : Total Primary Energy Demand of the EU 2005-2030 (Reference and Alternative Policy Scenarios)

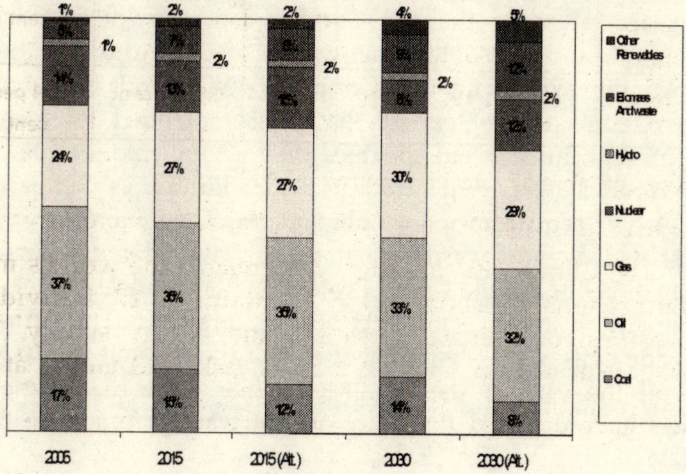

The European and in particular the Italian and German industries see currently little choice but to build new, more effective and environmentally clean coal plants to replace ageing infrastructure, to compensate phasing out nuclear power and to guarantee the base-load of electricity consumption for a 24 hours electricity supply.

Table 10.3

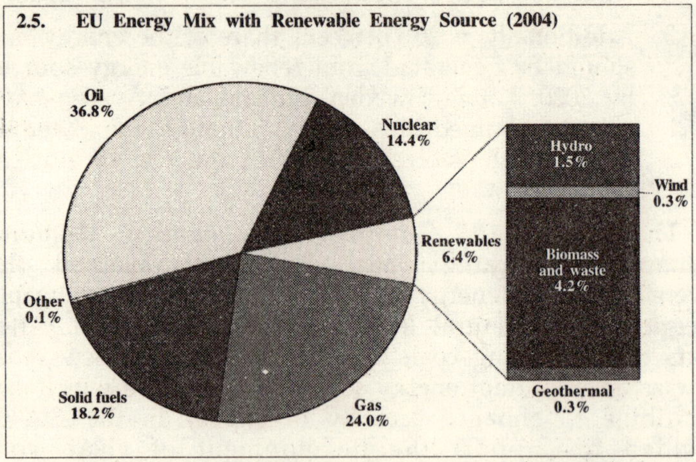

Source: *Commission Staff Working Document – Key Energy Policy Data,* Brussels, 10 March 2007

EU member states have also begun to re-think the nuclear option as the EU Commission, the International Energy Agency (IEA), the Energy Information Administration (EIA), the World Energy Council (WEC), and numerous international energy experts have recommended for years. At present, nuclear energy does play a vital role. In 2004 it produced 31 per cent of electricity in Europe as compared to 14 per cent from renewable sources. The Green Paper of 2000 had already warned that the EU would not meet its obligations under the Kyoto Protocol without nuclear energy. Annually, it avoids some 300 million tonnes (mt) of carbon dioxide emissions — equivalent to half the amount produced by all the cars in the EU. Meanwhile most EU member states have declared that they do not want to renounce the nuclear power option. For economic, environmental, technological, and political reasons, the nuclear power option is also undergoing a worldwide renaissance.

10.1 Europe's Energy Supply Security and its dependence on Russia

Since November 2000, the European Commission has warned in its first 'Green Paper' that in the next 20-30 years, upto 70 per cent of the Union's energy demand (presently 50 per cent) will have to be imported. With regard to oil, EU's dependence could reach upto 90 per cent, for gas 70 per cent, and for coal 100 per cent.

EU members possess only about 0.6 per cent of the world's proven oil reserves, 2.0 per cent of the global gas reserves and, at least, 7.3 per cent of proven coal reserves. With its eastward extension, the EU has only been able to increase its coal reserves substantially (by 41 per cent), but not its oil and gas reserves. In 2004, the EU-27's total primary energy supply was generated by oil (38 per cent), gas (24 per cent), solid fuels (18 per cent), nuclear energy (14 per cent), and renewables (6 per cent). Despite the projected expansion of renewable energy sources upto 20 per cent of the EU's overall energy mix by 2020, the new capacity in future will predominantly be generated by fossil resources with a rising percentage of gas, whilst the number of oil and solid-fuel power stations will continue to decline.

With regard to the EU's future energy supply security, the expansion of natural gas as an environmentally clean energy source will be the most problematic factor in the next two decades for EU member states. Europe is already the largest natural gas import market and will continue to be till 2030. But today, almost half of the EU's gas consumption is being imported from only three countries: Russia (23 per cent), Norway (14 per cent), and Algeria (10 per cent). Given current trends, gas imports would increase to 81 per cent over the next 25 years. By 2030, Europe would have to import 488 billion cubic metres (bcm; in comparison, North America 159 bcm and China/India just 85 bcm), if the gas demand would not be mitigated. The projected additional imports of gas are ranging from 50 bcm up to 300 bcm till 2030. The share of gas in total primary demand will simultaneously rise from 24 per cent by 2005 to 32 per cent by 2030. In the future, a growing share of EU gas imports could be shipped as Liquefied Natural Gas (LNG) which would offer better crisis stability for gas imports as shown in Table 10.4 currently, only France, Spain, Greece, Italy, Belgium and Portugal have LNG import regasification facilities.

Table 10.4: European Natural Gas Imports from Russia in 2005 (in per cent)

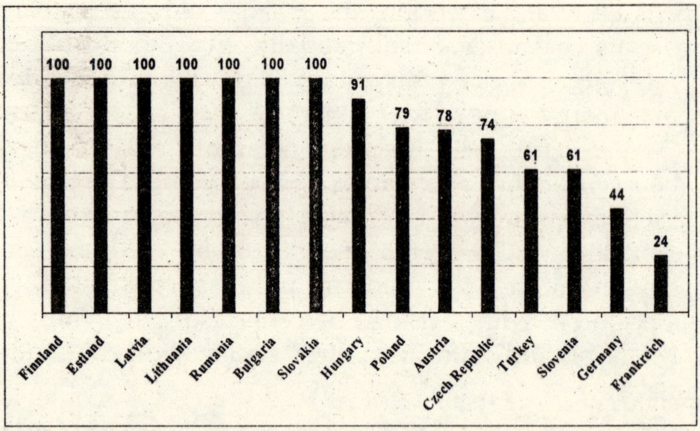

Source: *EU, IEA, Eurostat, 2005.*

10.2 The EU-Russian Energy Partnership at the Crossroads

In many ways, Russia seems to be the natural energy partner for the EU. It holds the world's largest natural gas reserves (48 trillion cubic metres), the second largest coal reserves, the eighth largest oil reserves, and is already the world's largest exporter of natural gas, the second largest oil exporter and the third largest energy consumer. At present, Gazprom alone supplies almost 25 per cent of the EU's natural gas needs, and the EU buys 70 per cent of

Russia's oil and gas exports (or two-third of Gazprom's total exports).

For modernising and expanding its energy sector, Russia needs more than US$ 900 billion by the year 2020. In this respect, the EU appears as the perfect modernisation partner of Russia. The supposed mutual interdependence on energy, trade and investments has been seen as the major strategic factor in EU's relations with Russia. This strong mutual interest and interdependence suggests that energy is an ideal sector in which relations can progress significantly. Success in the energy sector could serve as a model for other areas of common interest. Russia's ongoing privatisation of its electricity sectors, for instance, still offers very good investment opportunities for the European energy industries.

Given the political instabilities in the Middle East, the natural solution for Germany and the rest of the EU seems to be to expand imports of oil and natural gas from Russia for satisfying its rapidly growing energy demand. At first glance, there are indeed a number of persuasive reasons (not least the argument of improved political stability) for a drastic escalation of energy imports from Russia, being the EU's fifth largest trading partner (after the US, Switzerland, China and Japan). However, the results of the "Thematic Groups of the Energy Dialogue" and the newly created "EU-Russia Permanent Partnership Council (PPC)" on Energy convened in December 2006 to address energy strategies, forecasts and scenarios and other cooperation issues had been limited and rather disappointing due to differing strategic interests on both sides and Russia's re-nationalization policies of its energy sector.

Furthermore, Russian energy export policies, in particular pipeline routes (which are often determined by geopolitical considerations rather than just an economic calculus), are still seen in the Kremlin not just as a tool of its economic/energy policies but also as one of its very few effective foreign policy instruments to preserve and maintain its "strategic interests" in neighbouring countries which are either highly dependent on Russian energy sources or function as important transit states.

The close cooperation between the Kremlin and Russian energy companies (particularly Gazprom) of enhancing pressure on Western energy companies to gain full control over Sakhalin-2 from an international consortium led by Shell (based on "unfair" contracts at the beginning of the 1990s in the Russian perception) and forcing TNK-BP to sell Gazprom the majority share (63 per cent stake) in the license for developing the huge Kovykta gas field (estimated to hold 2-3 tcm) in June 2007 has not only threatened its international reputation, but also future Western investments. In this context, the EU has been unsuccessful in persuading Russia to pursue a market-oriented energy policy or in aligning the "EU-Russian energy partnership" with market principles.

But the previous Russian government under President seemed to be sure that the world in general and the EU in particular had no other choice in times of tight energy world markets and sky-rocketing prices for oil and gas than to cooperate with Russia in asymmetric energy relationships and "world sellers' markets, in which the producers' side had the last word.

10.3 Russia's Looming Gas and Oil Crisis and its Implications for the EU

While the EU views such partnership realistically rather than as a long-term vision, simultaneously it has become increasingly uncertain whether Moscow will be able to increase its total gas exports beyond 180-200 bcm by 2020 and beyond. In 1991, natural gas accounted for 42 per cent of Russia's energy. This has increased to more than 50 per cent during the last few years. Furthermore, the present European gas imports are coming from older fields, which are depleting rapidly, whereas many new gas fields are located in Sakhalin and Eastern Siberia and are expected to offer better gas export prospects for China, Asia and even the United States in the future.

Officially, Gazprom plans to increase its gas exports to Europe up to 220 bcm by 2020 from the present 157 bcm. By that time, new fields are expected to account for nearly 50 per cent of all gas produced. But given its falling production levels from 2006 (557 bcm) to 2007 (548 bcm) and its ambition to raise its gas output by 20 per cent by 2020, this increase will be difficult to achieve without the acquisition of new assets inside and outside Russia.

As a result of failing investment in the exploration of new gas fields, confirmed by the IEA, a deficit of gas supplies is expected in Russia and Europe of up to 100 bcm per year in 2010 compared to actual demand. Russian officials have repeatedly confirmed its gas deficit. Its present success of its energy foreign policy and of its gas diplomacy thus stands in sharp contrast with its emerging domestic gas crisis and with the series of deadly explosions in communal networks and limitations on gas supply in many regions during last winter.

If one includes Russia's independent gas producers' capability, Russia's gas production was originally expected to rise from an estimated 608 bcm in 2003 to 655 bcm in 2010 and 898 bcm in 2030 (IEA in 2004). It was hoped that net exports of gas would increase from 169 bcm in 2002 to 182 bcm in 2010 and 274 bcm in 2030. But this forecasts was a best-case scenario, which has become increasingly unrealistic during the recent years. The rising EU gas import demand could only been covered by gas imports from other countries and regions such as Norway, the Middle East, Central Asia/Caspian Sea region and Africa. In other words the EU would be forced to diversify its gas imports anyway.

At first glance, the EU seems to be in a very favoured position. Unlike any other region of the world, the EU is geographically surrounded by many gas-exporting countries. Eighty per cent of the global gas reserves are within a range of 4,500 km; most of these reserves can be connected to the EU by pipelines. However, most of those gas export countries are considered politically unstable. With these energy supply challenges confronted, the EU has recognized that it needs an active and coherent energy foreign policy at the regional and global level.

10.4 Rising EU-Competition with Russia in Central Asia and the Caspian Region (CACR)

Russia has presently two major objectives in its pipeline and oil and gas export policies:

1. One, it builds new oil and gas pipelines (such as North Stream or the Baltic Pipeline System/BTS towards Ust-Luga in the Gulf of Finland) as well as oil and gas export facilities through the Black and Baltic Seas to Germany and the "old EU" in order to avoid "problematic transit states" and to diversify its export routes.
2. Two, it tries systematically not only to undermine the EU's Nabucco gas pipeline project (the first independent one from Central Asia to the EU directly without going over Russian territory), but also the EU's wider diversification plan for its future gas supply (such as increasing imports from North Africa or the Middle East).

Russia's recent policies towards improving its bilateral ties with Hungary, Austria, Italy, Greece and Bulgaria are part of a larger strategy to undermine a common European policy towards Central Asia in particular the Nabucco-pipeline project, which is of crucial importance for the EU's energy security and the diversification of energy supply. By circumventing Russian pipelines, the Nabucco project would result in a "loss of money and strategic influence" for Russia. From Moscow's perspective this could potentially trigger an "energy crisis". In that context, German and EU policy-makers have overlooked two important facts:

First, independent gas pipelines from the Caspian region to Central Europe would constrain Russia to invest in the exploration of new gas deposits in their own territory. This, in turn, would secure long-term Russian as well as European gas supply.

Second, the Russian focus on gas imports from Central Asia is due to geopolitical reasons and contributes to the "gas crisis" in Russia. Moscow has thus become a less reliable energy supplier for Europe.

The sequel of the EU Spring summit of March 2007 has seen European energy companies, with the backing of their respective governments, develop closer relations with Moscow. Short-sighted national interests are threatening a unified approach to the EU's external energy policy. At the same time, Russia has increasingly become dependent on gas imports from Central Asia and the Caspian region (60-80 bcm) to meet its domestic gas consumption and maintaining high-price exports to Europe. At present, one-third of all European gas imports from Russia are supposed to come *de facto* from Central Asia. Even Gazprom's investment programme for 2008 with US$ 30 billion is going into new transport routes (such as Nord and South Stream[1]), storage facilities and trading hubs rather than into the development of new gas fields and repair of the existing old pipelines. Both pipelines, Nord Stream and South Stream, are expected to be commissioned around 2013. But their resource base remains doubtful particularly with regard to the South Stream pipeline, which is somewhat overlooked in the EU's discussions. Neither Russia nor Central Asia (including Turkmenistan) currently posesses the 31 bcm a year for the South Stream pipeline. The Nabucco and the South Stream pipelines compete with each other for Central Asian gas resources, overlapping transit routes, and national markets of individual EU member states in Central and South Eastern Europe along those routes.

---

1 The South Stream Pipeline should preempt the Nabucco transit route and circumvent Ukraine's transit pipeline network system. It will run from the Russian Black Sea coast across the seabed of Bulgaria and from there in two different directions: one going southern toward Greece and Italy, and another northern to Serbia, Slovenia, Hungary and Austria.

Russia's tactic of "divide and rule" the EU and its national energy champions by offering the status of a "hub" and the extension of the South Stream pipeline to their respective territories has triggered an undeclared contest among the EU member states for the best bilateral deal with Gazprom for future supplies and South Stream gas and storage sites. Although Austria's proposal to include Russian gas for the Nabucco project is not the most preferable option for Gazprom, it would totally change the overall strategic objective of the Nabucco pipeline: building the first gas pipeline from Central Asia (Azerbaijan) via Turkey to Europe by circumventing Russian territory and breaking Russia's gas pipeline monopoly in Central Asia for European gas imports. Supported by its government, the Austrian company OMV as the project leader of Nabucco has defected from the EU's top priority pipeline project by joining Russia's South Stream project in February 2008 as well as by turning the Baumgarten terminal and gas hub near Vienna into a fifty-fifty basis joint venture (re-designated as the Central European Gas Hub/CEGH) with Gazprom under agreements signed in November 2007 and January 2008.

10.5 EU's Efforts of Reducing its Gas Dependence on Russia

Given the results of the March summit and the agreed targets for 2007, new studies have predicted a much lower gas import demand of the EU till 2030. If the EU successfully reduces total European energy demand by 20 per cent by 2020 and obtains 20 per cent from renewable energy sources, it would significantly reduce the EU's overall energy demand as well as its gas demand and imports from Russia. In 2005, the EU's combined gas production with Norway amounted to nearly 300 bcm, which will decrease to 200–250 bcm till 2030. Between 2005 and 2006, the IEA had already reduced its forecasts of the EU's rising total gas imports in 2030 from 530 to 488 bcm. In the future, they might be somewhere between 350–450 bcm (317 bcm in 2005 by EU-27) to compensate for the decline in domestic production and the increase of demand. The reduced gas demand forecast is also the result of the fact that many new EU member states are already increasing their own coal production and consumption which has become cheaper than importing Russian gas. It also coincides with their supply strategies to reduce their dependence on Russia and to diversify their gas imports.

Furthermore, the Greensteam-pipeline from Libya to Italy, becoming operational in 2008, will transport 9 bcm. With increased production from Norway to the EU, Norway's exports will rise from 84 bcm to 125–140 bcm annually. In addition, the announced LNG projects would represent an additional import capacity of about 100 bcm per year after 2010. These alternatives will give the EU more bargaining power vis-à-vis Moscow. In order to strengthen its energy supply security, the EU has gone ahead with a number of pipeline and LNG projects to import non-Russian natural gas from sources other than the planned Russian-German Nord-Stream pipeline (2 x 27.5 bcm = 55 bcm).

Table 10.5: Main Greenfield Pipeline Projects.

Project	Supplier	From	To	Capacity (Bcm)	Investment (M €)	Foreseen Start-Up
Medgaz	Algeria	Hassi R'Mel	Spain	8–10	1300	End 2008
Galsi	Algeria	Hassi R'Mel	Italy	8–10	1200	2009–2010
ITG-IGI	Caspian	Greece	Italy	8–10	950 (IGI)	2011
Langeled	Norway	Ormen Lange	UK	22–24	1000	2006–2007
Nabucco	Caspian	Turkish Border	Austria	25–30	4600	2010
Total additional non-Russian gas supply capacity via pipelines to Europe: 71 – 84 bcm						

Source: *European Commission 2007b: 24.*

Despite its engagement policy of "Verflechtung" (building interlinkages) with Russia, even Germany has strengthened its diversification of gas imports. Thus companies like E.on Ruhrgas or VNG, which have close strategic ties with Gazprom, will import much more gas from Norway and are planning a LNG terminal in Wilhelmshaven. Furthermore, Germany's second largest energy company, RWE, has become an official member of the Nabucco-project.

Turkmenistan has offered 10 bcm for 2009 and beyond, Iraq will deliver 5 bcm at the beginning of 2011, and Egypt has promised another 2 bcm starting at the end of 2009. In this context, it is important to note that Kazakhstan and Turkmenistan have increased their official proved gas reserves. Kazakhstan has added an estimated 35 trillion cubic feet (54 per cent increase over 2006 proved reserves) and Turkmenistan 29 trillion cubic feet (+41 per cent towards 2006). Although Turkmenistan under its current contracts sells 42-44 bcm gas a year to Russia, its new government under President Guurbanguly Berdimukhamedov is much interested in diversifying its exports at real market prices, including to Europe.

Summary and Perspectives

During last year, Russia's approach has been most visible in its efforts to undermine a common European policy towards Central Asia. Moscow tries to torpedo the Nabucco-pipeline project, which is of crucial importance for European energy autonomy and the diversification of energy supply, with a rival pipeline ("White Stream-pipeline") and to maintain and strengthen its gas pipeline monopoly from Central Asia to the EU member states. The resulting pipeline rivalry in Central and South Eastern Europe between the EU and Russia has led to increasing tension between the recognized need for a common EU energy and gas market and individual EU member states acting in their own declared long-term (but in reality short-sighted) energy security interests. This tension is at the core of a growing European rift over how to deal with Russia and its newly induced self-confidence as the self-declared energy superpower of the 21st century who can exploit the asymmetric energy dependencies of the EU and its individual member states on Russia.

Despite its huge progress on the way to adopt a common energy (foreign) policy as part of the Energy Action Plan, the EU is now confronted with four major challenges in the months and years ahead:

1. First, the public debate about the results of the Spring summit concentrated on the "historic agreement on climate change". This rather narrow focus, however, jeopardizes the balance within the energy triangle between security of supply, competitiveness and sustainability. A one-sided orientation toward climate issues leads to a marginalization of the other two objectives, namely competitiveness and security of supply and, therewith, an inability and lack of attention to cope with many of the above mentioned global and geopolitical challenges.

2. Second, EU heads of states and governments have failed to agree upon a common strategy towards Russia, the bloc's most important energy supplier, as part of its declared energy foreign policy. Since the EU's March 2007 summit the lack of coherence in the bloc's external energy policy has enabled Russia to continue successfully with the "bilateralisation" of energy partnerships with Austria, Italy, Hungary, Greece, Bulgaria and Serbia at the expense of the other members of the EU and the EU itself. Thus Russia has still been successful in adopting its traditional politics of "Divide and Rule!" and to play off individual European states and their "national energy champions" against each other.

3. Third, if the Nabucco-pipeline is not be built, the new EU member states in Eastern Europe will largely

remain dependent on Russian gas imports. In this case, a common regional and liberalized EU energy market (particularly for gas) seems hardly realistic. It will rather be fragmented and fractured, which would undermine the EU's objective to create a liberalized European energy market and a common EU energy policy and strategy. Moreover, it would also have inevitably negative consequences for the EU's Common Foreign and Security Policies (CFSP) and speaking "with one voice" towards Russia and other important partner states. Of course, such a fragmented and fractured regional energy market would also be in the future the best playing field for Russia's "divide and rule" strategy towards the individual EU member states and their energy companies. However, it is definitely not in the EU's long-term strategic interest.

4. Finally, Russia currently attempts to encircle the EU and cut it off from alternative imports of gas from North Africa and Iran. On July 12 and 13, Gazprom CEO Alexei Miller visited Teheran and signed a memorandum of understanding for joint ventures for the exploration and development of gas and oilfields. While Moscow has no interest that Iran is developing nuclear weapons, it is equally not interested in successful negotiations to find a settlement to the nuclear conflict. If such a peaceful accord could be worked out between the West and Iran, then the EU and its energy companies would immediately start close energy cooperation with Iran (having the world's second largest oil and gas reserves), in particular related to gas pipeline projects. In this case, Russia would not only loose important market shares in the EU gas market but also its most relevant foreign policy instrument and leverage in the EU.

On July 9, Miller offered Libya to buy up the entire oil, gas and LNG production designated for exports in the coming years. By coordinating Libya's energy exports with Gazprom marketing those exports in Europe, Libya may benefit from Gazprom's enormous profits in Europe. A similar Russian proposal was made to Algeria in 2007 and as recently as in the beginning of July to Azerbaijan. However, neither Algeria nor Libya nor Azerbaijan have made any commitments so far. It remains doubtful whether these gas partners of Europe would see such a Russian monopolization of their exports to Europe in their long-term energy security interest and would not damage their increasing economic-political ties with the EU. Nonetheless, the EU needs to avoid a proactive preventive strategy using all diplomatic and economic means to ensure that such a Russian encirclement strategy will be successful.

For the time being, the EU-Russian "strategic energy partnership" will have to focus on improving energy efficiency and conservation on the Russia side as well as on closer technological cooperation with regard to renewable energy sources. If these working programmes are successfully implemented, they would contribute to the energy security of Russia as well as of the EU. But this new focus is also an indicator that the most wanted and needed cooperation between the EU and Russia, namely in the gas field, is hampered considerably by the very different strategic interests on both sides. They are the result of Putin's re-nationalization policy in the Russian oil and gas sectors and his energy foreign policy in a political alliance with the "siloviki" at home by using energy and pipeline dependencies of other states for promoting defined Russian strategic interests in order to rebuild its previous great power status.

11

Political Economy of Energy Cooperation in Northeast Asia

Jae-Seung Lee
(Korea University)

11.1 Energy Crisis and Energy Security in Northeast Asia

Persisting high oil price since the mid-2000 brought a sense of crisis to Northeast Asian energy security. Northeast Asian countries—China, Japan and Korea—suffered from the global shortages of energy supply and their rising foreign dependence of energy supply. The International Energy Agency (IEA) forecasted that energy supply problem in Northeast Asia would become even more serious in the future.[1]

[1] International Energy Agency, *World Energy Outlook* (2002)

Table 11.1 : Outlook of Energy Demand in Northeast Asia

(Units: MTOE, million tons of oil equivalents)

	1999	2005	2010	2015	2020	Average Yearly Increase (per cent)
China	797.5	1,072.5	1,377.5	1,720.0	2,110.0	4.7
Japan	537.5	572.5	605.0	635.0	665.0	1.0
Korea	182.5	240.0	267.5	300.0	325.0	3.6
Taiwan	78.6	97.3	110.7	126.1	142.6	2.8
Southeast Asia	1,596.1	1,982.3	2,360.7	2,781.1	3,242.6	3.3
World	9,547.5	10,965.0	12,315.0	13,792.5	15,287.5	2.3

(Source: *IEA, World Energy Outlook, 2002)*

Energy crisis in Northeast Asia has often been attributed to its heavy reliance on the Middle Eastern energy production.[2] Korea and Japan have depended on the Middle Eastern oil for more than two-thirds of their energy supplies[3] and any supply shock arising from the political and economic instability in the Middle East will have amplifying effects on these countries. As a consequence, their energy security will always be exposed to involuntary supply instabilities.

However, recent energy crisis is not a solely attributed to the Middle Eastern factor. Rapidly increasing Chinese energy demands are another important cause of energy

[2] Mamdouh G. Salameh, "Quest for Middle East Oil: The US versus the Asia-Pacific Region," *Energy Policy*, Vol. 31, No. 11 (September 2003).

[3] In case of petroleum, the three Northeast Asian countries' (Korea, China, and Japan) dependence on the Middle East is almost reaching 75 per cent (Korea 77 per cent, Japan 86 per cent, China 53 per cent).

crisis in Northeast Asia as well as at the global level.[4] To sustain its fast development, a stable supply of energy sources—especially oil and gas—became essential for the Chinese economy and its aggressive efforts for energy procurement may potentially lead to a friction with its neighbouring countries.[5]

Instability in Southeast Asia may pose another danger for energy security because the region serves as an important energy transportation route. Many Northeast Asian countries depend the oil and LNG transportation on the route passing the South China Sea, but the Strait of Malacca is also known as a source of territorial disputes between neighbouring countries. Piracy and terrorism pose another security threat in this region.

The North Korean factors are also related to energy security in Northeast Asia. The energy crisis in North Korea has led to an overall shutdown of industrial activity and in turn a total economic crisis. The energy crisis also have triggered political and security crises including its nuclear program.

11.1.1 Energy Cooperation in Northeast Asia

Amid the growing threats of energy security, the importance of Northeast Asian energy cooperation has been consistently

---

[4] Robert A. Manning, *The Asian Energy Factor: Myths and Dilemmas of Energy, Security, and the Pacific Future* (New York: Palgrave, 2000).

[5] International Energy Agency, *China's Worldwide Quest for Energy Security* (OECD, 2000). For the impact of the China factor, see Keun-Wook Paik "The Implications of China's Gas Expansion towards Natural Gas Market in Asia" *Chatham House Paper* February 2004; Pablo Bustelo, "China and the Geopolitics of Oil in the Asian Pacific Region," Elcano Royal Institue Working Paper No. 38/2005 (September 2005); Roland Dannreuther, "Asian security and China's energy needs", *International Relations of the Asia Pacific* (August 2003); Felix K. Chang, "Chinese Energy and Asian Security," *ORBIS : A Journal of World Affairs*-45, 2. (2001)

emphasized in recent years.[6] The objectives of Northeast Asian energy security cooperation include the stable energy procurement through the enhanced relations with Russia, the formation of energy institution in Northeast Asia, the formation of consumers' cooperation (Korea-China-Japan) and devising cooperation mechanism to resolve North Korean problem. Interests for energy supplies took the largest portion of these discussions.

So far, there have been both governmental and non-governmental discussions about energy cooperation in Northeast Asia. Government level discussions include Senior Officials Meeting on Energy Cooperation in Northeast Asia, in which UN ESCAP is involved. UN ESCAP SOM adopted the Khabarovsk Communiqué in October of 2001 and the Energy SOM and Working Group were installed. In April of 2003, the Vladivostok SOM agreed on holding *Intergovernmental Steering Committee of Senior Officials* regularly. *Intergovernmental Council on Northeast Asia Energy Cooperation* was officially established in Ulaanbaatar, Mongolia on November 17th, 2005 under the supervision of UN ESCAP. Korea, Russia, Mongolia and North Korea participated in this institution.[7] The *Trans-Asia Energy System*, recently launched by UN ESCAP, is another effort to search for regional energy cooperation at a Pan-Asia level. Non-government discussions include various academic and research institution-led projects and specific development projects at the private company level.

---

6 Doh, Hyun-Jae, "Energy Cooperation in Northeast Asia: Prospects and Challenges," *East Asian Review* 15, 3 (Autumn 2003).; Selig S. Harrison, "Toward Oil and Gas Cooperation in Northeast Asia", Asia Program Special Report (December 2002).

7 However, Japan and China do not participate officially and it still lacks a comprehensive utility. Inducement of Japanese and Chinese participation will be pivotal for further progress of this institution. The fact that representatives from China and Japan were absent shows the political limitation inherent in an organization for Northeast Asia energy cooperation.

At a broader East Asian level, several regional institutions currently function as a framework of East Asian regional cooperation, and energy discussions within these institutions cover energy issues encompassing Asia-Pacific and East Asia.[8] In APEC, the Energy Ministers' Meeting has been held on a regular basis. The ASEAN—plus three—Energy Ministers' Meeting has also been held consistently.[9] ARF also began to discuss energy security and energy cooperation at the regional level.[10]

However, participating countries share little understanding on common goals and the mechanism to facilitate cooperation are not fully established yet. Until this point, it is true that Northeast Asian energy cooperation has progressed without the institutional support that would serve to mediate differing interests among the participating countries. Even though various forms of cooperation are currently underway and have made certain progress, realistically speaking, the status of Northeast Asia Energy Cooperation is still at the beginning stage of bringing the issue to the table rather than solving the problem.

11.1.2 Geopolitics of Northeast Asia Energy Cooperation

Geopolitical structure of Northeast Asia is basically inclined to be competitive rather than cooperative, and the participating countries need to find out cooperative elements among this competitive structure. The cause of the energy competition can be found in the region's uneven distribution

---

8 Siddharth Varadarajan, "Energy key in the new Asian architecture" (January 25, 2006) (http://www.globalresearch.ca/index.php?context=viewArticle&code=VAR20060125&articleId=1802)

9 Andrew Symon, "Energy and ASEAN Economic Integration", *Regional Outlook* (2005/2006)

10 Jae-Seung Lee, "Energy Security and Northeast Asian Cooperation," Paper prepared for the Second Meeting of the CSCAP Study Group on Asia Pacific Cooperation for Energy Security, Goa, India, September 14-15, 2007.

of energy resources.[11] In a situation in which energy supplier is limited to Russia, inter-state competition on the distribution of resources between three big consumers—Japan, China, Korea—has been increased, which was well manifested in the recent conflict over East Siberian oil pipeline route between China and Japan.[12]

Northeast Asian energy cooperation is also likely to be influenced by political and security environment. The primary factor that hinders Northeast Asia Energy cooperation is the political and security instability in the region. Even though some risks have dissipated since the end of the Cold War, the risk factors still exist among Northeast Asian countries, especially between South and North Korea.[13] Also, the Sino-Japanese relations and Japan-Russia relations have hidden sources of territorial disputes and other political conflicts. Political instability exists not only internationally but also intranationally in the region, and such instability acts as an obstacle in establishing a stable cooperative organization in the long run.

Because Northeast Asian nations have different interests in the energy agenda, and do not share common understanding of the ultimate goal of energy cooperation, there are many difficulties in establishing an institution for regional energy security. Many obstacles of energy security cooperation come from the lack of strong political will of the governments involved.

---

11 Glada Lahn and Keun-Wook Paik, "Russia's Oil and Gas Exports to North-East Asia", *Chatham House Paper*, April 2005.

12 David Murphy and Martin Fackler, "Asia's Pipeline Politics," *Far Eastern Economic Review* (July 24, 2003); Kent E. Calder, "China and Japan's Simmering Rivalry", *Foreign Affairs*, (Mar/Apr 2006).

13 Fereidun Fesharaki, "Energy and the Asian Security Nexus," *Journal of International Affairs*, 53, 1 (Fall 1999).

11.1.3 Prospects of Northeast Asian Energy Cooperation

Under a complicated political environment, it is irrelevant to ignore such political and security factors in pursuing energy cooperation.[14] However, it is also unreasonable to directly project inter-state competition into the energy cooperation schemes. Diverse forms of energy cooperation and discussions should be continually promoted so that they could create building-blocs through various channels.[15]

Considering the current Northeast Asian situation, short-term expectation on comprehensive energy cooperation would not be optimistic. The momentum of regional cooperation is still weak in Northeast Asia to induce active energy cooperation. On the other hand, the breakthrough of the energy cooperation alone may not fully drive Northeast Asian regional cooperation. Meanwhile, the propulsion of politically non-sensitive projects would be achievable as a cooperation agenda at the intergovernmental level. Apart from political relationship, private sector cooperation projects have been and will be consistently pursued. Nonetheless, political support will be needed when those projects face existing diverse obstacles.

11.2 Conclusion: Policy Recommendations

11.2.1 Enhancement of Bilateral Relations in Northeast Asia

Constructive restoration of bilateral relationship will be the primary condition for sustainable Northeast Asian energy

---

14 Amy Myers Jaffe, "The Potential of Energy as a Geopolitical Binding Factor in Asia," *Post-Soviet Geography and Economics* 42, 7 (October/November 2001).

15 Energy-related cooperation may show different features according to the nature of following issues: upstream and downstream project; strategic reserve (partial); joint procurement; joint mechanism for the management of oil/gas pipeline; cooperation in energy-related international organization (e.g. IEA).

security cooperation. Enhancement of bilateral relationship with Russia will be the fastest way to secure energy supply for energy importers in Northeast Asia. Furthermore, building a cooperation mechanism among the consumer countries, notably China, Japan, and Korea, needs to be pursued simultaneously. Enhanced bilateral relations among these consuming countries are the essential elements for effective cooperation. In the long run, dialogue on energy strategy between producing country and consuming countries should be activated.

11.2.2 Expanding the Geographical Scope of Energy Cooperation

For an actual progress in energy cooperation, the scope and the focus of Northeast Asia Energy Cooperation should be expanded and diversified. The agenda for energy cooperation should first be shared by Far Eastern Russia, Northeastern China, Japan, and North Korea. However, energy agenda sometimes crosses over the limited regional scope. The energy strategies of Russia, China and Japan do not focus solely on Northeast Asian as a target area. Furthermore, the identity as "Northeast Asia" of those countries is weak.

Under the situation that inner dynamics and institutional basis of Northeast Asia Energy Cooperation are not strong enough, the scope of multilateral energy cooperation may have to be expanded to the level of East Asia and Asia-Pacific region. In some cases, Central Asia and Southeast Asia could also have a strategic importance.

11.2.3 Multilateral Linkage of Energy and Regional Cooperation

Under the stalemate of bilateral relationship, detour approach through multilateral cooperation can be effective. Overall regional cooperation should be enhanced in the sense that regional cooperation can eventually be foundations for Northeast Asian energy cooperation. Comprehensive economic cooperation, such as FTA, would have significance in this perspective. Energy security issues can also be placed on agenda within the scope of East Asia and Northeast Asia security cooperation.

Progress in Northeast Asian and East Asian cooperation provides external environment directly influencing Northeast Asia energy security cooperation. If regional cooperation makes rapid progress, Northeast Asia energy security cooperation can also be implemented at the accelerated pace. On the other hand, if regional cooperation does not make much progress, energy cooperation may lose its dynamism.

11.2.4 Focus on the Soft Cooperation Agenda

As discussed earlier, current political environment in Northeast Asia is not favourable for large-scale energy development projects. Regarding both hard security issues and energy supply issues, Northeast Asia countries are competitors rather than cooperative partners. However, energy security cooperation of small scale regarding soft agenda such as an enhancement of energy efficiency, strategic reserve and joint R&D projects can be implemented as pioneering projects. The prospect of this soft energy cooperation is optimistic in that it is linked with the soft, non-traditional security cooperation which has shown a steady progress in recent years at the Asia-Pacific and East Asian level. Focusing on the softer side of energy security cooperation is not less important and, foremost, much more feasible than sensitive development projects which would accompany huge political and economic risks. A starting point for Northeast Asian energy security policy, therefore, should be the choice of practical and achievable energy security agenda.

Bibliographical References

Bustelo, Pablo, "China and the Geopolitics of Oil in the Asian Pacific Region", Elcano Royal Institue Working Paper No. 38/ 2005 (September 2005)

Calder, Kent E., "China and Japan's Simmering Rivalry", *Foreign Affairs* (Mar/Apr 2006)

Chang, Felix K. "Chinese Energy and Asian Security," *ORBIS: A Journal of World Affairs* 45, 2 (2001)

Dannreuther, Roland, "Asian Security and China's energy needs", *International Relations of the Asia Pacific* (August 2003)

Doh, Hyun-Jae, "Energy Cooperation in Northeast Asia: Prospects and Challenges," *East Asian Review* 15, 3 (Autumn 2003).

Fedorovskiy, Alexander, "The North Korean Nuclear Crisis and Russia", *International Journal of Korean Unification Studies*, vol.14 no.1 (2005)

Fesharaki, Fereidun. "Energy and the Asian Security Nexus," *Journal of International Affairs*, 53, 1 (Fall 1999).

Harrison, Selig S., "Gas and Geopolitics in Northeast Asia : Pipelines, Regional

Stability, and the Korean Nuclear Crisis," *World Policy Journal*, 19, 4 (2002/03)

International Energy Agency, *China's Worldwide Quest for Energy Security* (OECD 2000)

Jaffe, Amy Myers, "The Potential of Energy as a Geopolitical Binding Factor in Asia," *Post-Soviet Geography and Economics* 42, 7 (October/November 2001).

Lahn, Glada, and Keun-Wook Paik, "Russia's Oil and Gas Exports to North-East Asia", *Chatham House Paper* (April 2005)

Lee, Jae-Seung, "A Framework of Analysis for the Establishment of Northeast Asian Energy Community," *IFANS Policy Research Series* (February 2004)

____________, "Energy Security and Northeast Asian Cooperation," Paper prepared for the Second Meeting of the

CSCAP Study Group on Asia Pacific Cooperation for Energy Security, Goa, India, September 14-15, 2007.

Manning, Robert A., *The Asian Energy Factor: Myths and Dilemmas of Energy, Security, and the Pacific Future* (New York: Palgrave, 2000)

________________, "The Asian Energy Predicament. *Survival*, September, 2000.

Murphy, David and Martin Fackler, "Asia's Pipeline Politics," *Far Eastern Economic Review* (2003.7.24.).

Paik, Keun-Wook, "The Implications of China's Gas Expansion towards Natural Gas Market in Asia" *Chatham House Paper* (February 2004)

Salameh, Mamdouh G. "Quest for Middle East Oil: The US versus the Asia-Pacific Region," *Energy Policy*, Vol. 31, No. 11 (September 2003).

Stern, Jonathan, "Gas Pipeline Co-operation between Political Adversaries: Examples from Europe" *Chatham House Paper* (January 2005)

Symon, Andrew, "Energy and ASEAN Economic Integration", *Regional Outlook* (2005/2006)

Tian, Chunsheng, "Sino-Russian Energy Cooperation and Geo-Strategic Issues", *China & World Economy* (May/Jun 2005)

Varadarajan, Siddharth, "Energy key in the new Asian architecture", (January 25, 2006)(http://www.globalresearch.ca/index.php?context=viewArticle&code=VAR20060125&articleId=1802)

12

Technology Developments in Energy Security

Alvin Chew

12.1 Introduction

Energy security has featured prominently in recent periods and has made it to the top agenda of both national and international policies. The current historical peaks in energy commodities have caused concerns for both developed and developing countries, as well as resource importing and exporting nations.

The intricate link between energy and the development of economies cannot be understated, whereby it is evident in the past that energy are drivers in many aspects of national developments. The energy component is significant in the development of strategic military capabilities down right to operational business transactions. Energy, to a certain extent, is the centre of gravity (COC) to which military strategist Clausewitz coined it as the hub whereby everything else is dependent on.[1]

The complexity involved in producing energy is central to the entire security issue. Often viewed as a fungible product in the economic sense, its finite resources have played a significant role in the shaping of foreign policies.[2] The phenomenon of global excessive demand with respect to the limited supply of fossil fuels has attributed to the current experience of high oil prices. In the technological aspect, energy is seen as an indestructible component.[3] Its unique characteristic of 'not being able to be created nor destroyed' has fundamentally led to the notion of sustainability, whereby alternatives and renewable sources are likely to feature prominently in the energy mixes.

This paper addresses the technological components of securing energy, in a globalised world whereby technology is increasingly employed as the solution to almost any problem encountered in the present era. It deals with the various aspects of improving the security of energy resources, and discusses some of the technological innovations made in these areas for policymakers to reflect upon.

12.2 Technology in the Exploration of Existing Oilfields

Oil is regarded as one of the fuels that has the quickest liquidity. It is primarily used in the transport sector, which in many countries, typically accounts for a large portion of their energy consumptions. The perceived knowledge that current oil production capacity is limited and will not suffice

---

1 Carl von Clausewitz, *On War*, translated by Michael Howard and Peter Paret, (Princeton: Princeton University Press, 1984), p569.

2 Daniel Yergin, "Ensuring Energy Security", *Foreign Affairs*, March-April 2006.

3 In physics, the law of conservation of energy leads to the phenomenon that energy cannot be created or destroyed.

with the expected growing demands from developing economies such as China and India has been challenged. It has been argued that fossil fuel such as oil is indeed available to see us for a much longer period, taking into account projections of growing demands.[4] The impeding factor is primarily the exploration techniques that are employed to locate oil reservoirs in other untapped regions.[5] Not only are there untapped regions for future explorations, better sensing technologies, such as 4D seismic imaging sensors, are developed to assess the changing dynamic conditions of current oilfields so as to provide more accurate measurements of available oil in the existing reservoirs.

The exploration techniques are nevertheless expensive, and oil companies remains hesitant to adopt better drilling techniques and oil exploration capabilities in their strategic plans. However, with the rising oil prices and alternative fuel sources, the oil industry would see the need to remain competitive so as to cushion the possibility of an impending oil shock, as witnessed in the past. A recent survey indicated that the market sentiments had pushed drillers to increase their oil production capacity, in contrast to adopting a long term plan for energy conservation.

12.3 Technology in Alternative Fuel Sources

In looking at alternative energy sources, the primary issue of sustainability deals with energy materials that are able to be reprocessed over a longer time period as compared to fossil fuels. Such a concept will alleviate the stresses in the global markets for fossil fuels as nations become less dependent on them to produce energy.

One of the renewables that has gained momentum is in the use of biofuels. As with many new technologies, the

---

[4] "World Oil Supplies are Enough for 'Many Decades' – Saudi Arabia's Al Naimi", *Forbes*, June 22, 2008.

[5] "Geopolitics and Geology Force Oil Companies to Explore New Options", *Scientific American*, May 28, 2008.

inefficiency associated in converting one unit of biofuels to energy does not make the first generation of biofuels a viable energy resource. Moreover, various contentious issues have cropped up with the use of biofuels as now food crops are grown for energy rather than for consumption, hence exacerbating the present global situation for high prices in food.[6] Technology has been developing in this area whereby it looks into improving the conversion of the raw products into energy, as well as looking for plants and crops that are not meant for food consumption. Furthermore, technological developments are also looking into more non-conventional growing methods of crops that do not require arable land, and hence freed up the shortage of land as well as deforestation that could have other serious repercussions on the environment.[7]

Another alternative for fuels is to tap into the natural forces, such as wind, hydropower, and geothermal energy. In a country like Singapore, which has limited territorial space but is situated near the equator, solar power would be an attractive alternative to consider in its future energy mix. Solar energy, which is initially deployed as heat for water heating systems, can now be harnessed into electricity with large-scale grid of photovoltaic (PV) cells.[8] With the current high oil prices, it definitely poses a strong motivation to develop PV cells that are commercially attractive to the masses. Another attractive feature of solar energy is its ability to be stored in the form of heat at a relatively low

6 Joachim von Braun, "Rising Food Prices – What Should be Done", *International Food Policy Research Institute (IFPRI) Policy Brief,* April 2008.

7 Peter Fairley, "Growing Biofuels – New Production Methods Could Transform the Niche Technology", *MIT Technology Review,* November 2005.

8 Kevin Bullis, "Large-Scale, Cheap Solar Electricity", MIT Technology Review, June 2006.

cost, or even as electricity that incorporates storage mechanism in the PV grid systems.

Alternative fuel resources are welcomed as these resources would serve to stabilise the markets for conventional hydrocarbons. However, while technological developments could pave the way for more products to be converted into energy, it must take into account several factors that do not alter drastically the existing conditions. The challenge remains still in improving the efficiency of alternative resources to feature them as a bigger proportion in global energy mixes,[9] but also needs to bear the consequences of other possible effects, such as environmental impacts and societal concerns, that could surface and affect the security issues.

12.4 Technology in Improving Supply Chains

The sources of energy are not readily available everywhere, and thus needs to be transported or distributed to locations whereby it can be harnessed for further use. It therefore remains crucial for the distribution of energy, in the form of raw materials or as a final output of power, to be delivered efficiently to the desired destination. Technology development is pivotal in these aspects so as to ensure both the reliable supply of energy materials.

The first aspect covers the physical security of the distribution chain. The security of energy supplies can be enhanced with the implementation of advanced technological solutions. For example, surveillance devices can be installed to monitor possible sabotage of the supply chains, be it the pipelines that carry natural gas or power cables that deliver electricity to homes.[10] Physical security is not limited to stationary infrastructure, but also mobile transportation

---

[9] International Energy Agency, *Deploying Renewables –Principles for Effective Policies,* 2008

[10] Richard Sia, 'Agencies See Homeland Security Role for Surveillance Drones', *Congress Daily,* December 12, 2002.

services such as oil tankers that channel through strategic locations. Surveillance of such activities, monitored via satellites, can help deter or overcome physical activities that could cause disruption in the supply chains.[11]

The second aspect is to improve the efficiency of delivering energy resources. In the case of pipelines, research can be done to prevent the loss of transmission of energy materials when passing through the pipelines. For power cables, the use of more advanced materials such as fibre optics could possibly result in fewer loss of power during the transmission process.

Technology can also be developed in changing the modes of transportation, or refining the energy products to suit a particular form of delivery. Taking the conventional example of transporting gases via pipelines, which imposes geographical challenges as well as political ramifications, the liquefaction of natural gases enables the product to be transported via LNG road tankers or sea vessels.[12] Similarly, compression of the natural gas into CNG would also serve as an efficient fuel source in the transportation industry.

12.5 Technology in Energy Efficiency and Conservation

Energy conservation is a low-hanging fruit that strives to maximise the potential use of energy resources. A large part of energy conservation is due to the change in societal mindsets, but in the technological domain, innovative systems can feature significantly in striving to achieve higher levels of energy efficiency.

Energy efficiency or conservation does not explicitly change the components of the raw materials, or rather its production stages. The transformation occurs in developing end systems that actually requires less input of energy to gain the desired output. For example, 'intelligent' buildings

---

[11] John Croft, 'Securing the Straits', *C4ISR Journal*, March 2007.

[12] Energy Information Administration, *The Global Liquefied Natural Gas Market: Status and Outlook*, December 2003.

can incorporate smart technologies for its systems, such as algorithms for its lifts or escalators, heating and cooling systems of the buildings, as well as sensor technologies for automated lightings. Modern buildings can consume less energy with the use of innovative materials for its façade, state-of-the-art equipment and electrical appliances.[13]

In the field of mobility, the engines of the car can be made more fuel efficient with research and development. New engines can also run on hybrid system that utilises both petrol and CNG tanks. In addition, fuel cell cars can be developed to improve their performance to match conventional cars. Take the case of Airbus A380. The aircraft is made on advanced technology: it carries more passengers, which obviously means more weight, consuming 12 per cent less fuel as compared to other aircrafts. Normally, it is more weight, more fuel but in the case of Airbus A380 there is a paradigm shift: more weight at less fuel[14].

An important technological development in the energy conservation is also analogous to the diversification of fuels resources. In the broad sense, energy security looks into the diversification of various types of fuels to achieve a more balanced energy mix in the nation's consumption. Similarly, at the user end, systems need to be compatible in order to accept the broad spectrum of fuels available in the future. An example at the individual level would be the production of 'green' cars on the road that not only accept petrol, but are also able to run on biodiesel and also other forms of fuels in the future.[15]

---

[13] Torcellini et al., 'Zero Energy Buildings: A Critical Look at the Definition', Conference paper presented at ACEEE Summer Study, California, August 2006.

[14] 'The Solution to Growing Air Travel', Airbus Economics. Also available at htttp://www.airbus.com/en/aircraftfamilies/a380/economics.html

[15] "The Road Ahead", *The Economist*, September 4, 2008.

Furthermore, energy conservation is closely associated with the concept of sustainability. As with the front end of energy production, the next generation of fast-breeder nuclear power reactors would accept the reprocessed fuel, this will achieve a tremendous savings of the spent fuel generated.[16] When we apply the similar concept of energy conservation at the user-end, large industrial systems that requires massive input of fuels for their operation, such as the steel rolling industry, can shave off considerable amount of energy inputs with advance systems that allow feedback of its by-products that are generated during the process.

12.6 Technology versus Cost

The world is more confident of progressing at a much faster pace mainly due to the advent of technology. Almost every problem looks to technology as a primary solution, if not, a force multiplier. The advantage reaped from acquiring leading edge technology is exponential, and therefore developed nations are likely to increase the technological gap *vis-a-vis* developing nations.

However, technology does not come cheap. It is intertwined with market forces and therefore nations need to be prudent when it comes to investing in the right technology. Usually, a premium has to be paid for the launch of a new product, and naturally dies off when it adjusts itself to the market conditions owing to increasing production and improvements in the performance of the system. Similarly, in the field of energy, the high oil prices had created a global sentiment to push alternative sources of energy to be developed, and also at the same time, propelling research on improving end-systems that could accommodate other types of fuel sources.[17] One can only

---

[16] Peter Dyck and Martin Crijns, "Rising Needs – Management of Spent Fuel at Nuclear Power Plants", *International Atomic Energy Agency Bulletin*, Volume 40, No.1, March 1998.

[17] "The Future of Energy", *The Economist*, June 19, 2008.

look to history and analyse that the rate of the development of solar energy had increased during the oil crisis in the 1970's, and subsequently research activities on solar power stagnated in the late 1980's when oil prices reverted to below US $10 per barrel.

In the spirit of interdependence, nations should collabourate to effect the sharing of technical know-how in order to hedge the risk in the acquisition of new technologies. The research of new technologies by developed states is primarily in competitive areas of strategic importance, such as the military or the space domain, whereby the concept of independence or supremacy is desired. However, energy is a common good that has now been driven mainly by market sentiments. Based on the concept of supply and demand, it might be more viable to adopt the interdependence approach, as in the way gas contracts are being negotiated. The EU is dependent on Russia for its gas supplies,[18] but the converse is also true as Russia will not benefit if there is no buyer for their natural gas. Hence, technology developments in the energy sector could possibly be more effective when regions or nations work together to share their expertise, rather than re-inventing the wheel.

Conclusion

Although technologies are progressing at a blinding rate, one important factor for its development in the energy sector is to take into considerations the possible downstream impacts it can generate in the future. The current era of interconnectivity would render a plethora of threats being turned into security issues. It is therefore crucial that the new developments of technology to address the current energy security issues will not lead to unrest in the regions.

---

18 Ariel Cohen, "Europe's Strategic Dependence on Russian Energy", *The Heritage Foundation Backgrounder #2083*, November 5, 2007.

One of the prime agenda the world is facing currently is the issue of climate change. The extensive burning of fossil fuels not only resulted in energy scarcity, but also carbon emissions that would cause disastrous pollution in major cities. Hence, technological developments have to pay attention to minimise the negative environmental impacts it could generate. It therefore needs to look into cleaner fuel resources, such as 'clean coal' technology and also fuel cells generated or hydrogen-powered cars that do not emit carbon. While nuclear energy is clean, the back-end issue is often contentious with the treatment of nuclear waste and the storage of spent fuels. Similarly, hydropower can also cause massive flooding and upset the ecological balance.

Food security, and subsequently high inflationary cost on commodities, arises owing to limited resources available. The incentives to grow crops for energy rather than food had aggravated the situation. Technological development in these areas should try to minimise the global poverty problem that the world could be grappling with.

Finally, technology collaboration among nations should be promoted so as to foster more effective technology transfer. As technology is often tied to cost, it can be perceived that the non-homogeneity of economies in a region could be a barrier for collaboration. Nevertheless, collaborative mechanisms can be forged based on varying economy of scales, whereby the largest investor is entitled to have a bigger proportion of the intellectual property. Ultimately, fiscal and technology policies provide the environment and conditions for technology transfer to be effected.

13

Energy Security: The Role for Nuclear Energy

Jor-Shan Choi

Epigraph

The growth in global energy-demand and the increased recognition of environmental impacts of carbon dioxide emissions from fossil fuel plants have created a sense of urgency for energy security and made many in the nuclear community to anticipate a return to significant growth of new nuclear power generation in the coming decades. If there is a resurgence of nuclear power generation, what is the role it can play in energy security, and what are the technical, institutional, and societal issues that must be resolved? We learn from past peaceful nuclear activities that significant safety and security incidents, and concerns associated with waste management and nuclear proliferation had resulted in a decrease in public acceptance for nuclear power in many countries. There is often an assumption that stopping nuclear power is the most effective way to minimize proliferation and stop the accumulation of nuclear wastes. That is not necessarily the case. A few countries have no nuclear power plants but pursued to develop sensitive fuel cycle technologies (enrichment and reprocessing). There is already an accumulation of global spent fuel inventory in excess of 230,000 MT as of 2000, and is projected to 900,000 MT by 2050. A return to substantial new nuclear power must satisfy a number of well-described criteria: plants must be economical, safe, and provided by adequate resource and infrastructure; the nuclear energy systems must minimize waste production, be proliferation-resistant, and be acceptable to the public; and financing for these capital-intensive plants must be made available. Also, with a combination of new reactor technology and coordinated, global fuel cycle services, a vision for a new nuclear regime could be set which could play a key role in meeting future energy demands while simultaneously reducing the proliferation, security and waste management challenges below where they are today.

13.1 Nuclear Power Today

Global nuclear energy capacity is currently about 372 gigawatts, with approximately 439 nuclear power reactors operating in 30 countries. Three countries account for one-half of all nuclear power reactors: the United States (104), France (59), and Japan (55)[1]. Nuclear energy currently accounts for about 16 per cent of the global electricity consumption. Most of the growth in nuclear energy occurred following the oil shocks of the 1970s. The low cost of uranium also helped make nuclear energy attractive. Nuclear energy development, however, began to retard after the Three Mile Island (1979) and Chernobyl accidents (1986) and after a drop in natural gas prices in the 1990s made gas-powered turbines more attractive than nuclear alternatives

[1] Power Reactor Information System (PRIS), as of December 31, 2007, IAEA

in Europe and the US. Nonetheless, nuclear energy has been able to maintain its share of electricity generation largely through standardization of design and operation, and by better plant management to achieve higher efficiency and availability.

13.2 Why Nuclear and Why Now?

13.2.1 Oil and natural gas prices

Sharp increases in oil and natural gas prices have made nuclear energy more attractive in the last few years. Whereas oil was priced at below $10 per barrel in 1999, it rose above $140 per barrel in June 2008. Natural gas prices have increased to more than double in June 2008 from the price of about $6.00 per MMBtu in December 2007. In the US and Europe, new electricity generation in the 1990s was fired by natural gas, but this is now changing.

13.2.2 Global climate change

The Kyoto Protocol to the UN Framework Convention on Climate Change entered into force in 2005, establishing legally binding levels for reductions in greenhouse gas emissions of an average of six to eight per cent below 1990 levels between the years 2008–2012[2]. Due to the perceived adverse impacts to their respective economies, major countries using coal such as China, India and the US have not yet abided to the limit set by the Kyoto Protocol. Nuclear energy, relative to fossil fuels, contributes little to greenhouse gas emissions. To eventually achieve the goals of the Kyoto Protocol, nuclear energy must play an important role in the world's energy mix.

13.2.3 Energy Insecurity

Recent suspensions have underscored the instability of the oil and gas supply. In 2006 a natural gas price dispute between Russia and Ukraine resulted in a temporary

---

2 Kyoto Protocol to the United Nations Framework Convention on Climate Change, Entry into force on 16 February 2005.

suspension of natural gas supplies to Western and Central Europe. In 2007, price disputes between Russia and Azerbaijan and between Russia and Belarus caused a temporary stoppage in oil supplies to Russia from Azerbaijan and from Russia to Germany, Poland, and Slovakia. Many states are wary of depending on imported energy sources, leading states such as France and Japan to rely on nuclear power for most of their electricity needs. Already, China, Japan, and India are seeking to secure long-term uranium contracts to support nuclear expansion goals. Relative to oil and gas, the ability to stockpile uranium offers greater assurance of weathering potential suspensions.

13.2.4 Raise the standard of living

Energy is the engine for economic development which contributes to the raising of the standard of living. The industrial revolution which started three centuries ago lifted the living standard of Western Europe, North America and other developed economies. It is the same yearning for raising the living standard that propels the economic drive in China and India, and soon for the rest of the developing world. So far, the carbon fuel cycle is the main engine for these economic developments, and we now know the potentially devastating effects on the environment due to the back-end of the carbon cycle. Nuclear energy is the proven technology which can provide a large scale electricity generation base for lifting the standard of living in many countries without emitting green house gases and further damaging the global environment.

13.3 Challenges and Opportunities

Despite its contributions and anticipated great potential, nuclear energy stands at a crossroad, facing significant challenges in terms of costs and financing, safety and security, human resource and infrastructural development, spent fuel and radioactive waste management, and nuclear non-proliferation. Although these are intractable techno-institutional-political challenges to the peaceful use of nuclear energy, recent advances in reactor design and operation, regulatory practices, and progress in international framework proposals have presented opportunities for the expanded applications of nuclear energy to meet the growing global energy demands.

13.3.1 Costs and Financing

The various factors involved in cost and financing are as follows:

1. **Challenges:** Building nuclear power plants is capital intensive requiring stable regulatory policy, skilled work force and infrastructural support, and long-term committed investment. In the past few decades, nuclear power construction and operation have proven to be poor investments, producing far more expensive electricity than originally promised. To evaluate nuclear power's future, it is critical to understand the costs and the risks of this technology. This is specifically true for a deregulated electricity environment where investors will increasingly share the financial risks of underperformance of generation assets.
2. **Opportunities:** In the US, the Energy Policy Act of 2005 and the Advanced Energy Initiative of 2006 sought to allay the investment risks by offering financial incentives for new plant construction that employs new reactors and technologies. Current nuclear plant operators have given notice that they intend to apply to the US Nuclear Regulatory Commission (NRC) for approval of 27 new "generation III+" reactors. These advanced reactors are of simplified design with many components factory-built and delivered to the plant site which cut the construction and generation costs. Also, passive safety systems using natural circulation are employed to enhance response to unanticipated accidents.

The comparison of the levelized cost for a typical coal plant, an advanced combined-cycle natural gas plant, a wind plant, and a nuclear plant to be built in the US is shown in Table 13.1. The wind option is included for comparison purpose realizing that the intermittent technologies like wind and solar produce less power over time than the other generating options. These cost estimates are based on assumptions used in EIA's *Annual Energy Outlook 2006*, expressed in 2004 dollars per mega-watt-hour[3]. The Table 13.1 indicates that nuclear generators are expensive to build, but their fuel costs are low; while combined-cycle gas plants are far less expensive to build, but their fuel costs are much higher. Without the inclusion of CO_2 charges (i.e., some form of carbon tax), the combined-cycle gas plant is the least-cost option and the nuclear plant the most expensive. Recent cost studies by the nuclear industry indicated that the Gen-III+ reactors can achieve a cost saving of 30 per cent over Gen-III reactors due to the reduced plant site footprint, reduced building volume, and less construction materials used.

Table 13.1 : Levelized Cost Comparison of New Generating Capacity in the US

(2004 Dollars per Megawatthour)

	Technology			
Cost Element	Coal	Natural Gas	Wind	Nuclear
Capital...	30.4	11.4	40.7	42.7
O&M...	4.7	1.4	8.3	7.8
Fuel.....	14.5	36.9	0.0	59.3
Total[a]...	53.1	52.5	55.8	59.3

[a] Includes transmission hookup costs.
O&M = operations and maintenance.
Source: *Energy Information Administration, Annual Energy Outlook 2006, DOE/EIA-0383(2006)* (Washington DC, February 2006).

[3] *The Annual Energy Outlook 2006*, Energy Information Agency, USDOE.

13.3.2 Safety and security

The various factors involved in safety and security are:

1. **Challenges:** Since the TMI accident in 1979, no new nuclear power plants have been built in the US for 29 years. The Chernobyl accident in 1986 also cast a long shadow and chill in the global nuclear business. The terrorist attack in the US on 11 September 2001 also raises awareness for significant security provision on nuclear facilities.

2. **Opportunities:** Since TMI and Chernobyl, the global nuclear power generation has maintained good safety record through stringent regulation, automated and redundant safety systems, and the industry's commitment to comprehensive safety procedures. Continued vigilance and independent regulatory authorities to maintain a competent safety culture are still required to keep nuclear power plants and their communities safe.

Since 11 September 2001, the nuclear industry has substantially enhanced security at nuclear plants requiring extensive security measures in place to protect the facility from intruders. Every nuclear power plant in the US has a detailed plan for responding in the event of an emergency. Utility companies test that plan regularly, with the participation of local and state emergency response organizations.

13.3.3 Human resource and infrastructural development

1. **Challenges:** The nuclear industry is currently in need of skilled workers, including welders, craft labour, technicians, engineers and scientists, to support construction and operation. Also, 40 per cent of the current nuclear power plant workers are eligible for retirement within the next five years. Furthermore, only 8 per cent of the current nuclear

plant workforce is under 32 years old[4]. There is much competition from other industries for graduates, and therefore, the nuclear industry must become creative if it is going to entice these graduates to enter and remain in the nuclear field.

In spite of the ambitious plan for new nuclear plant construction, the fabrication of the reactor pressure vessel could be a bottle-neck due to the limited availability of the nuclear-grade large-ring forgings that are currently only available from one Japanese supplier (Nippon Steel Works). This potential shortfall significantly affects the construction schedule and could be a project financing risk.

2. **Opportunities:** One of the most important elements of human resource development (HRD) is the activity of universities. The number of students in nuclear engineering has decreased in the western world since the late 80s with the drop of construction of nuclear power reactors. In the US, the number of university nuclear engineering programs has reduced to about 30 now, less than half of the number in 1980. Fortunately, there is currently an upturn in student enrollments in nuclear engineering, and new courses on nuclear energy have recently established in several universities. Governments have also increased the nuclear research funding to universities. In the US, DOE funded the Nuclear Energy Research Initiative (NERI) with strong university participation. In Japan, the MEXT supported the Nuclear Education and Research Initiative (NERI) activities in the Global Center-of-Excellence (G-COE) program at Tokyo University in 2007. The activities encompass the curricula in nuclear technology, radiation applications, and nuclear sociology to support basic technology fields such as material corrosion, welding technology,

[4] A. Stall, Florida Power & Light Company, Keynote speech made at the ANS 2007 Annual Meeting.

radiation beam applications, and so on, and to sponsor students for opportunities to experience first-hand the societal aspects of nuclear energy uses. In addition, a standing committee composed of government, university, and industrial companies was organized to discuss the issues on human resources to minimize the imbalance between demand and supply.

There has been a significant structural change of the nuclear industry over the years. Instead of the dozen companies building reactors in western countries in the 1980s, there are currently 3 major consortia building LWRs. These are: Toshiba/Westinghouse, General Electric/Hitachi, and Areva/Mitsubishi. Operating in a mature industry, these consortia work with their supply chain for major equipment, including reactor pressure vessels, steam generators, moisture separators, and re-heaters, etc. to support the near-term deployment of Gen-III and Gen-III+ reactors.

13.3.4 Spent fuel and radioactive waste management

Spent fuel and radioactive management too have challenges and opportunities.

1. **Challenges:** Currently, spent nuclear fuel (SNF) and/or high-level radioactive wastes (HLW) are accumulated on or off reactor sites in water pools, in steel or concrete-and-steel dry canisters, pending final disposal in geologic repositories.

2. **Opportunities:** Ultimately, radioactive waste (HLW and/or SNF) will be disposed of in geologic repositories. Several countries have begun their national repository programs at specific or generic locations. Although repository technologies and approaches pursued by countries are site-specific, the challenge to repository development is institutional and political. To obtain public and

stakeholders' acceptance and support for a repository site location, it is important that:

1. the program-need must be convincingly established,
2. roles and responsibilities of stakeholders must be clear,
3. respect for societal consent must be apparent,
4. decision making process must be transparent and open, and
5. the program must be robust with possibility of alternating or reversing course.

In 2002, the US Congress approved Yucca Mountain, Nevada, a remote desert location, as the site for a centralized deep geologic repository for SNF and defense HLW. On 3 June, 2008, the US DOE submitted to the USNRC the license application for a geologic repository at Yucca Mountain.

It is important to recognize that a repository is not merely a nuclear waste dump, but a solution to the global non-proliferation issue because it is in the interest of the international community that there is a final acceptable solution for the safe and secure disposal of spent-fuel and/or radioactive wastes.

13.3.5 Nuclear non-proliferation

Following are the challenges and opportunities of nuclear non-proliferation.

1. **Challenges:** Following the nuclear weapons tests by India and Pakistan in May 1998, the terrorist attack in the US on 11 September 2001, and the nuclear weapons test by North Korea in October 2006, there was a high level of concern for state-based nuclear proliferation and terrorists acquiring nuclear explosives. The discovery of covert nuclear programs in Iraq, North Korea, Libya, and Iran (and perhaps,

in Syria), and the exposure of the A Q Khan. Pakistan-centred black market weapons network also alerted the world that something must be done to curb the spread of the sensitive technologies associated with the nuclear fuel cycle, namely enrichment and reprocessing.

2. **Opportunities:** To stop the "onward proliferation" and to prevent the nuclear weapons, materials, or capability to fall onto the wrong hands, several world leaders [IAEA Director General M. ElBaradei (2003)[5]; US President Bush (2004)[6]; Russian President Putin (2006)[7], etc.] had proposed to limit the enrichment and reprocessing operations either under multinational control; or to states that already have full scale functioning plants; or in a regional fuel cycle center. An expert group on nuclear fuel cycle, commissioned by IAEA advocated a multinational approaches (MNA)[8] and suggested to:

    1. reinforce existing commercial market mechanisms on a case-by-case basis through long-term and transparent arrangements with government backing,
    2. develop and implement international supply guarantees with IAEA as guarantor of service supplies, e.g., a fuel bank, and

[5] M. ElBaradei, *The Economists*, 16 October 2003.

[6] The US President Bush's Speech to the National Defense University, 11 February 2004.

[7] On September 5, 2007, Russia's first multilateral nuclear fuel cycle enterprise — the International Uranium Enrichment Center in Angarsk was legally incorporated as a joint venture between Russia's Tekhsnabeksport and Kazakhstan's Kazatomprom.

[8] INFCIRC/640 — Multinational Approaches (MNA) to the Nuclear Fuel Cycle, 22 February 2005.

3. promote voluntary conversion of existing national facilities to MNA, including regional MNA based on joint ownership, co-management, etc.

History reveals that it is challenging to pursue multilateral approaches to prevent the spread of sensitive fuel-cycle technologies while promoting the peaceful use of nuclear energy for sustainable economic development with a reduced environmental burden. Recent events indicate the urgency for a global threat reduction effort to prevent state-based proliferation and terrorists acquiring nuclear explosives. "Business as usual" is no longer an acceptable option. We need a new nuclear regime to deal with the non-proliferation and environmental risks.

13.4 A New Nuclear Regime

Center to the new nuclear regime is the formation of a global network of nuclear fuel cycle facilities[9], as shown in Figure 13.1. In such network, reliable front-end fuel supply services, including conversion, enrichment, and fabrication for various fuel types are provided transparently and cost-competitively. Under certain cooperative arrangements, spent fuel discharged in the back-end can be taken back for interim storage and final disposition at locations operated by nuclear consortia and supported by their respective national governments. The objective for the network is to provide a "cradle-to-grave" nuclear fuel-cycle service to countries interested in producing electricity for their citizen.

[9] J. S. Choi, "An innovative fuel cycle concept with nonproliferation and waste considerations for small and medium sized reactors," International Seminar on Status and Prospects for Small and Medium Sized Reactors, Cairo, Egypt, 27-31 May 2001.

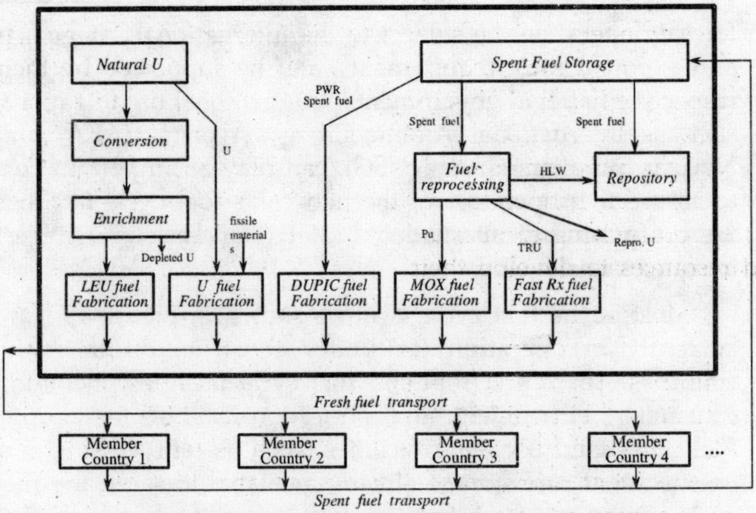

Figure 13.1 Global Network of Nuclear Fuel Cycle Facilities

The network would be an attractive option for new and emerging nuclear countries as they would have the assurance of reliable fresh fuel supply and timely spent fuel removal. These countries can benefit from nuclear energy without the burdens of non-proliferation concerns and management of nuclear wastes, much like a country can provide air transportation to its citizens by operating airlines without the large investment in aircraft manufacturing. The network would enhance nuclear non-proliferation because countries will have less incentive to acquire their own enrichment or reprocessing technologies if fresh nuclear fuel can be reliably supplied and the spent fuel removed.

The fuel cycle facilities in this global network are not necessarily owned by a country, nor need to be located in a "regional fuel cycle center". In fact, such a network could best be formed by commercial market mechanisms or contractual agreements between two or among a few parties (i.e., a nuclear consortium). Companies providing fuel cycle services must abide to international rules and regulations for safe operation, be subject to the international safeguards and export control requirements, and be supported by their respective national governments. International organizations, such as International Atomic Energy Agency (IAEA) and Nuclear Suppliers Group (NSG), can play an important role to assure that operators of the network's fuel cycle facilities are conforming to international safety standards and subject to safeguards.

Most of the fuel cycle facilities shown in Figure 13.1 are currently in operation (or under construction) in many countries. There are front-end fuel cycle facilities, including conversion, enrichment, and fabrication facilities for various fuel types, and back-end facilities, such as reprocessing and on-site spent fuel storage already available to serve the fuel cycle service needs. A few key facilities in the back-end fuel cycle, notably the regional spent fuel storage and waste repository are still absent for the global network.

After the consolidation of the nuclear industry in the sequel to Toshiba's acquisition of Westinghouse (particularly, the reshuffling of the relationships between western and Japanese companies), there is a trend that utility companies would prefer the supply of fabricated fuel as a package, rather than buying uranium, conversion, enrichment and fabrication services separately. These new commercial arrangements among the ranks of reactor vendors and fuel fabricators (Toshiba/Westinghouse, GE/Hitachi, Areva/Mitsubishi) are leading to stronger partnerships in offering a packaged fuel service. Big uranium suppliers, notably Kazatomprom with its acquisition of a 10 per cent stake in Westinghouse, are seeking integration to add value to their uranium asset. This new business arrangement open a new opportunity for commercial consortia (i.e., Toshiba/Westinghouse/Kazatomprom, etc.) to offer a "cradle-to-grave" fuel cycle service to emerging nuclear countries. Such service, possibly could include the reliable supply of fabricated fuel (by Toshiba/Westinghouse with uranium provided by Kazatomprom) to fuel the reactors, AP1000 built by Westinghouse, and the timely removal of spent fuel for storage at locations in Semipalatinsk, Kazakhstan. The plan for final disposition of the spent fuel could be decided by the owner-countries, the consortium, and their respective national governments. This "cradle-to-grave" fuel-cycle service could be attractive to countries with small nuclear power program and small amount of spent fuel because these countries may have limited resources to develop their own repositories for their spent fuel and radioactive wastes.

Not all countries can or are willing to provide the back-end spent fuel take-back services. Some may be able to do it easier than others. For instance, the nuclear weapons states as a whole operate more than 50 per cent of the world's nuclear electricity generation capacity, and holds more than half of the global spent fuel and radioactive waste inventories. They have to develop their own repositories and perhaps, could provide spent-fuel storage and waste disposal services to other countries within their region.

The former Soviet Union took spent fuel back from the Soviet-designed reactors located in Eastern Europe and Finland. Currently, the Russian Federation (RF) accepts spent VVER fuel from Commonwealth Independent States (CISs) for a fee and on a case-by-case basis. The US also takes back research reactor spent fuel from other countries on grounds of non-proliferation. Major uranium-producing countries such as Canada, Australia, Kazakhstan and others can help in dispositioning spent fuel from other countries. The return of spent fuel to the uranium supplying countries for disposition could enhance global security and non-proliferation, and simultaneously, benefit their respective uranium-supply business.

The importance of the global network of nuclear fuel cycle facilities is to relieve the burden of nonproliferation and wastes for countries/utilities operating nuclear reactors for electricity generation. It is by no mean a restriction to a country's own fuel cycle development. The network, if it can be formed, is only an option aiming at improving nonproliferation and radioactive waste management. If a country decides to develop enrichment and reprocessing, it should prepare to deal with the nonproliferation and waste issues in a manner conforming to international norms.

Conclusion

There is little doubt that nuclear energy will remain an important part of the global energy mix. The growing world population and the yearning for raising the standard of living in the developing world will keep the demand for energy strong for the foreseeable future. The recent price surge in oil and gas, and the recognition of environmental impact by the carbon cycle have prompted countries to diversify their energy sources. Nuclear energy is the proven technology which can provide a large scale electricity generation base for lifting the standard of living without emitting green house gases and further damaging the global environment. Currently, nuclear power is already helping the transportation sector by producing electricity to support a hybrid car industry. In the future, nuclear energy can also help offset transportation emissions through the production of hydrogen.

The G8 meeting in 2008 agrees on a new initiative to expand the civilian use of nuclear power to curb global climate changes[10]. Any expansion of nuclear generating capacity, however, would require the reactor vendors to keep nuclear energy as cost effective and safe as other alternative sources of electricity. It also requires the regulators to maintain vigilance and a competent culture for safe operation, as well the policymakers to take steps to mitigate the inherent risks of nuclear power, including non-proliferation and waste management.

The nonproliferation risks of a nuclear renaissance clearly depend on the shape of nuclear expansion. More LWRs pose

[10] An Article in *The Japan Times*, 1 July 2008.

essentially no new technical challenges to the current safeguards system, but additional enrichment or reprocessing capabilities in non-nuclear-weapon states could easily strain the system. The provision of "cradle to grave" fuel services as advocated by a global network in a new nuclear regime could go far toward limiting the spread of sensitive fuel-cycle technologies but still needs the participation of and decisions by key governments, such as the US and Russia, on spent fuel and waste disposition. Clearly, measures are needed to help shape these potential developments to minimize the proliferation and waste management impact.

Index